Praise for *The Crystal Text* by Clark Coolidge

"In *The Crystal Text* by Clark Coolidge, language is restored to its original grace. And what is the origin of language? Is it innovation? Does it subvert while instructing? This poem brings the written word to life. It was written in the 1980s, serving as a deep source for poets and all those who cherish literature. The poet spars with history, memory, and what it means to be fully human. The informative afterword is a rare treat."
—**NEELI CHERKOVSKI**, AUTHOR OF *THE CROW AND I*

"Like the mouth to a cave or mine, *The Crystal Text* offers the best entry to Clark Coolidge's writing. Here's a sui generis American poet, an eager amateur geologist, conversing with a mineral gifted to him, locating the surfaces along language that allow light's passage. Impossible to imitate, Coolidge tests the hardness of syntax, scratching new registers upon it to clarify human perception and the ways we lend it language."
—**EVAN KENNEDY**, AUTHOR OF *METAMORPHOSES*

"*The Crystal Text* is at once a philosophical poem in the lineage of Lucretius and a word-jazz excursion in the spirit of Monk and Lacy. Here, the poet's stylus becomes a drumstick that patterns a nonlinear logic of fleeting reflections, performing cymbal-clash as symbol-crash. The result is a unified field theory of music, thought, and poetry. The reissue of Coolidge's long out-of-print masterpiece deserves a standing ovation."
—**ANDREW JORON**, AUTHOR OF *OO*

T0151460

"There's a majesty in this book with a crystalline center that refracts and reflects this extended, wandering meditation on what it means to write and to be in the world. And there is also an ease and a luminous beauty and such a depth that this book remains resonant years after its original publication."
—JULIANA SPAHR, AUTHOR OF *THAT WINTER THE WOLF CAME*

"Summoned from a translucent bedrock made of equal parts diamond and table salt, snowflake and graphite, and operating a mineral eon or two away from the more obvious sorts of time, *The Crystal Text* affirms an irreducible poetic truth: small things are fathomless. Telluric, etheric, astral, whatever; for me, Clark Coolidge's achievement is in having sat down at his desk in 1982 and followed guidance—through boredom and rapture, through eddies of self-doubt and brain-fried waves of inspiration—to the great goal: new vistas of nowhere else."
—PAUL EBENKAMP, AUTHOR OF *THE LOUDER THE ROOM THE DARKER THE SCREEN*

THE
CRYSTAL TEXT

CLARK COOLIDGE

Foreword by Peter Gizzi

Afterword by Jason Morris and Garrett Caples

CITY LIGHTS BOOKS — SAN FRANCISCO

Cover photographs copyright © by Garrett Caples
Cover and text design by Patrick Barber

City Lights would like to thank Micah Ballard, Peter Gizzi, Andrew Joron, and
Evan Kennedy for their assistance in making this book.

Library of Congress Cataloging-in-Publication Data

Names: Coolidge, Clark, 1939– author. | Gizzi, Peter. | Morris, Jason. |
   Caples, Garrett.
Title: The crystal text / Clark Coolidge ; foreword by Peter Gizzi ;
   afterword by Jason Morris and Garrett Caples.
Description: San Francisco : City Lights Books, 2023.
Identifiers: LCCN 2023029803 | ISBN 9780872869042 (trade paperback)
Subjects: LCGFT: Poetry.
Classification: LCC PS3553.O57 C79 2023 | DDC 811/.54—dc23/
   eng/20230703
LC record available at https://lccn.loc.gov/2023029803

City Lights Books are published at the City Lights Bookstore
261 Columbus Avenue, San Francisco, CA 94133
citylights.com

CONTENTS

FOREWORD

BY PETER GIZZI

One often hears the words unique or original to describe an artist. But few poets have such a unique style, such original syntax, and such a signature sound within such a vast output of works in so many forms. Clark Coolidge has said in interviews that he is very sympathetic to the work of Beckett, Stein, and Ashbery. I mention their names because they illuminate Coolidge's sense of ambition for the language art, its scope and possibility for both the rigorous work of intellection and the reach for new aesthetic registers. As the poem tells us: "To grasp the relation of words to matter, / mind, process, may be the greatest task." When I sat quietly this morning and thought of words to describe Clark and his work, these came: magical, reaching, discovery, transformation, odd, generous, ecstatic, visionary, rigorous, loving, conceptual, exhilarating, syncopated, synchronic, hilarious, major, open, consumed, believing, surprising.

The Crystal Text is a masterwork, and one of Coolidge's most revered texts. It is the best example of his deep focus, his sense of scale, and seemingly endless expressive language. The story goes that Clark sat each day and meditated on a crystal that he kept on his desk and wrote what he received from this transmission. The result is an inspired crystallography, a deep meditation on time and mortality, on materiality and the mystical, on everything. And the writing is crystalline, faceted, and gives pleasure, as he writes: "The crystal is but one nexus in the drain / of speeded possibles." And while this poem can hone in on microscopic wiggy detail, ultimately its scale is cosmic.

Clark's work has been written about in myriad ways. Back in the late '90s I spent a day in the library to look up what had been said about his work and found he has been called, and I quote: *a minimalist poet, an experimental poet, a sound poet, a New York poet, a second-generation New York School poet, a gestural poet, a Jazz poet, a Steinian poet, a disjunctive poet, a Language poet, a maximalist poet, a vernacular poet, an abstract poet, an epic poet, a meditative-philosophical poet, a Kerouacian poet, an undisclosed narrative poet, a paratactic poet, a prose poet, a Beat poet, a formalist poet, a difficult poet, a poet's poet.*

Coolidge is a one-man avant-garde and has lived at an extreme frontier all his writing life. His dedication to the art of writing is total; for 50 plus years and counting, one can find him at his desk, literally every day. His output staggers. During the period of the mid-'80s and early '90s, when I was editing the journal *o•blēk*, I met a lot of poets and writers and I would invariably ask them who they read, or who should I read, or simply who their favorite poets were. And whether I asked James Schuyler, Robert Creeley, Keith Waldrop, John Ashbery, Charles Bernstein, Susan Howe, Barbara Guest, Michael Palmer, Rosmarie Waldrop, Michael Ondaatje, J.H. Prynne, Robin Blaser, David Shapiro, John Yau, Lyn Hejinian, Tom Raworth, Bernadette Mayer, or Fanny Howe—one name always came up, and unequivocally: Clark Coolidge.

THE CRYSTAL TEXT

"If only he could turn around, just once (but looking back would ruin this entire work, so near completion)"

—Rainer Maria Rilke
Orpheus. Eurydice. Hermes

He had his things all there, waiting for . . .
They had active possibilities. Should they be
enumerated, or left to breed? Knowing has
nothing to do with any of this. Any one could
know what he did. Any one could close the
door on them and walk downstairs and out leaving
them all untouched together.

Something appears on the screen, speech.
For your own sake at least stick to the subject.
But who could better care for things?
They come apart, and stay that way.
They are not dangerous to themselves.
He had the thought once that everything fit together.
If only he could remove himself sufficiently.
No, nothing but what comes from the inside this time.
Blind intervals.

They were surprised by the blue and red shower at night.
The next day the usual explanation.
They saw it. But what they remembered later
was that they had heard about it later.

You must take your mind off them to allow them.
Is this any more than a change of pronoun?
Writing that leaves things alone. In the room
unsorted the things were able to breed his
discontent later. Was his fate to
leave all things together untouched?

It's not just known what caused certain
things to happen. Maybe it's human.
Maybe it's *all* human. Maybe it's water.

"What if it were to . . . " is a deflective mechanism.
A mother and daughter. The hand on the air, that you
see but to hear.

The weather is yours, he thought.
The train smash. And the barrel of eels
in the desert.
The placenames all distractions
from anyone's key to will.

●

To grasp the relation of words to matter,
mind, process, may be the greatest task.
The batter. The worst of the winter.
What I discover in writing comes out of the
mess, the mix. I know no nodes before.
Don't move. Not a millimeter off the knowing it to be.
My imagination is not pure enough to present
the single beatific image. The spread beatitude of image,
the hose to the slaughter.

●

"History falls *outside* like snow."

●

The thought to weight things
and then rush back to them.

●

I hate history because it has never entered the
world as a life. It has no direction
but back into the fold. No touchingness
very following to its black boxes. I would
want to walk out and say, The History of
the World. I would need a stream through
my head like the quartz crystal in the sunshaft
on the desk of a following wood. I would
seek needs but not as if written down later,
I have a tiny sun patch hot on my skull and
am wandering and in my stumbling sundering the
swamp. I own no gloves for I have always
a pencil.

The world is not a laboratory for farming smells,
nor a wand for stretching watch words.
The hills intervene, that the lake's evening
sheen will not snap. The place of the hands
is in battle or surest love. The capsule of
termination is on the stove. The store and its light.

Senseless this arrival at a subject for a start.
I could watch the stars above a carbarn
or retreat from youth's retrieval. I could
mention an arsenal, or word I didn't mean
to swerve from, its meanings endlessly
elude me. An etude, or stored plant stand,

ballpark brand, car passing cattle. You were sure
of me then, that I'd by you bend again
and train the looseness of held hands to a
zenith pitch. Those that would not marvel
at a witch, but turn to Hawthorne for
unfiltrated solace and a carry-all nature.
Books that dry to a flatness of sky and will
never meet up under my aim. I twirl
my shirts to the flame of a blunted ambition.
No ripe ammunition has a terminus.

I bring this all down here now to end the time
and its harvest damages.

•

The light has escaped me, and now the
windows will fill.
Repetition an addition without evening
the score.
The names of people are not felt very well.
Whose is an *entire* name?
I reflect myself in the darkness
the world has made of me.
I am fascinated with the self
as it exists without one
active separation.
We are whole edges.
If I turn to sleep
the same one will urge tomorrow.
There are no capsule versions.
The crystals *are* the wall.

•

About all I was able to do
was introduce them all to the mess.

Recognizing all little of yourself in everybody
and a lot of yourself in somebody.
Friendship a quick blur, a sharped note.
In the fast and leftover strew
the mauling of counters to equal a straight light.

And the great mystical pull of things,
what do I think of?

•

The collections of solace have yet to see their binding.
And yet is the far away that stays.
Caught in the furthest stays, the stars.

The man with the shoe collection
has time for nothing.
The victim of clutch and sod.

Bright briars in the Avenue of Rhythms.
The celestite clicks itself against the finer substance of air.

Meanwhile, and over miles, we console ourselves with cut stones.
And somewhere a fire lights
far from here.

As conversation treats
of the gaps
fingering the whole part
of the air, the one
near your ear

The misgivings of solace
a stem flow
of your leaden futurity

I put the crystal
to my brow and turn.

•

Who were they out there through instruments
in the light? I didn't know and don't.
Perhaps I didn't wonder so much but now I do.
But then I do not realize who *I* am either.
Present time makes the stranger of yourself, whom
you do not have the charm of watching walk away.
How do I think of myself, having long had the practice
of never. A mirror? False view, always
behind the shine of one's own hands. To write
a long book of nothing "but looking deeply into oneself."
I feel this sentence turn on the flinch of a laugh.
A scorn, not for oneself probably but for the
possibility of a self view. Does it wait out there
in the black shine of spateless corridor world.

Large books are not for oval minds.
Handwriting is not a frame for the self.
A shocking caliber of words that would hoof
one off one's own best known path.
The prime abstraction of "one" seems necessary
to hold the self in the frame. And a life
of sentences in rooms one holds no plan to.
I dived at you, self, but you rubbed me blank
in all my own mirrors. Scorn. No one owns,
can possess, a mirror, the reflecting surface.
If I walk in the hallways I will first see
the light before I can identify what precisely
rejects it. This is not knowledge, but then
what is it?
I can see the largeness of the world in a
stone ledge I could then place in my pocket

for all the world's care. How many hunches,
that might prove out, there?
The crystal attains toward a transparency
my mirror approaches, face or no face.

●

Rearranging all the things into forms of face
pressed into the air. Not knowing what to be there,
nor budging from it. Image as negative
off the "real" world. Impression in what?
Vacuum of ignorance? I am accoutred
with knowledges. But they seldom make an
inroad. The image is what I have forgotten
the painter prized. It curls itself out of semblances
of silence and the unaccustomed nerve.
Bloat is the result of knowing and takes no hold.

The crystal brings sided air to a water standing.
Quartz is the original untampered word.
When I propose a live reading of poem I think of
going up there to cut some fine edges.

●

He sees the fire in the crystal
as a network of cracks in the air.
And the wood of its rest should flinch.
Or enbrown itself in rising heat.

The next thought of an ice cut gem.
A hand emblem that will not stay to hand
but drop off into endlessly pursuant space of all the angles.

A striated sharpness
a glow zone to the front of the skull
riot of realms unbudged in fix
slower than tooth, slower than any
belt of earth
apt to remain over at
one catch never closed
builded beyond builded
plane of the clocks
poured from the shock
strain invisible
tell it left-handed and bleed under the sign

●

The crystal is blonde and has no discernible edges.
A scrawl is all my writing, even to the ends
of the eyelashes. Any space one can see
is enclosed.

Do you wish this to seem a definitive space, having had
it follow something? That one is therefore
no longer here or there. High walls produce
deeper dreams.

How long has it been necessary to think?
You will stop now and watch a shiny black window.
Though nothing may come of it, the effect upon the
mind is necessary. Now, that aporian solid.

Bland events inspiring high style, you may leave.
It has been said. Knowledge of matter results
from meditation in between steps. The light
gets bent slightly, exactly which were the words?

I know you, you exist everywhere. The sentence
never to complete, no matter. I will lift
heavy weights in an undefined space of
dark blue lights, enveloping shadow, no more
tappings of the pavement.

Within no sentence but inside my mind
the name of a city. A spot not yet withered
with explanation. From which you neither
come nor go, I'll settle for that. A still
question, a statue with one arm, and it is time.

•

A prosewriter's mind's mass is thought plots
but a poet's is fielded of words.

What do you see when you look out with your language?
A pile of hooted buckets.
A loose laugh spoon.
Miles of adroited pain paper.
Lungs full of glass beads.
A list of nodules knowing of nameless.

These are never only things, just, but the words
retracked. Circling as a flying object almost home
with your pen above whatever oval tensions
or the wheat in your litmus class, the glow on the fear.
The witness motions are there. Or add another
e to that th.

How meditations stayed on the mountains for
the trees were too near. Close to the beer
and all it rhymes there. The habit to write.
And then the habit to forget all the while
trailing the hand so far, fraught with inner

and deeper like a movie calm with little light,
frostings of fluorescents on the inner casements
in a night so long and strong it nears an unprovoked
death.

He went backwards into the avenue learning his art
on tiptoe. All the women meanwhile in the sand
berating with tines. The time to take your self
seriously back. The numbers on the back referring
to nothing in garages or on the sound. I could
leak from the radio's cab remembering my youth,
reassembling the steady meadow or ledge on which
white coins were left. The precise book
closed out this section of the cold dream.

Why cigarettes, why anything, prepare them, and I
thought the noon siren given but it didn't.
Houses are at large and you don't come home
to the dentist. Everything's backwards in the
something of what I remembered writing of it.
The end of writing a conscionable step.
Up from woods of leaves and the ragged coming
winter. The Corningware on the fossil fire
and your tender new-lapped noun won't burn.
But it will fizzle and end up in a little but
packed book. Volumes of the rememberings of
friends, what they hated enough not to put in
letters but you found it and whirled it and
it's flush kept its place all this fell pounded
into rights time. The lashings that are avoided
by perfect lettering the first two letters
scribed in reverse order and faced up to just
as fine.

A pure writer's name in circuitous crystals
such as he would kneel to place on his clothes.
I could remember winter, said Melville,
stamping on his nib, but I won't do
precisely enough to delay its remove.
Reaching beeches and lettered arms. It lay there
on the page in an unprepared way the pen.
Ovals are amounting up to sun wells and the toad.
The picture a circle with inset head lines,
a reminder to have finished something last night,
the cat. Removal is the only sense of finishing
you get. The crawl you call your whole mind's
remove into thought. The world not a
circle, the face not. But the unwished mirror
could be an oval. Then recalling at the beach
a circle it was. I could remember you
but I'd rather you be here and done.

I'll have no liars here in the room of this
house of the sun just coming. I finished
the sonata, what a perfect thing to be able
to say, no one allowing as how but I'm just
doing it. I've done it and that I've said.
But the chill space sense that I haven't yet
written anything. I must though learn to
write bigger, if not (but I must, this) faster
as Picasso came to me in a dream with
the full moon in my face to say of painting.
I don't say anything I haven't learned from
you might be a nice thing to say, to think
if not repeat, the laughs come hard in
Auld Lang Syne.

Now the sun is starting to stop, coming out perhaps
turning so tiresome. We had to laugh all night
it was so needless. Today I will see someone

in my house that I haven't seen anywhere in a year
or more. His name is No One, or Harmonica,
or The Man Without One, or Milk of Magnesia
won't do you any better. Wherever the lights are not
on I will write there myself to sleep. To
rest under a brick of the whole School of
Arrival Tribe of Avenue and Restless Beginnings,
the whole goldsod history of the world in a
better butter remnant. I was stood up in a
chair, its name was Wrists Tied. Dreaming
of sundown in the noonhour's occulting shine.

Moonhair should be the verb. Then we'd all
itch just to stand still once for all the rest
of the language's personages and their houses.
Wilting on a road where the sun particles all turned
to wet. How much night could you get, thinking
of all the sun's appearances in every book on
one's shelf. The one there that is never singular
but waits out late in the sun's downpour dreaming
of roofs of the moon. You, not to be thought
underhanded but perhaps a bit much underhandled.
You wait to catch the sense of what I left
out on the track.

Behind myself always as Mrs. Findash
late for lessons below the primitive private school
deChirico chimney stack where pianos burned
in the ash of cold remnant attention, my
fingers the distance of one dream
from the keys to the solution of moreways else.
Something. Somethings are always burning.
Something always underattended, as
if boring but not till later under smallnesses
of attention. Never to be said to be the
end or least of anything. Always to be just

coming up on something in the sole glare of
daydrop. I don't care to recall all these
names I keep having.

Circular cat, replete with wavers, are you thought to be
carefully sad? or full-throated I would
keep to secrets lining my cap knowing you.
The ball came to rest in pale pall space, the
leaves diced into. The big book would perhaps
include me that I not be its flick of the wrist.   ·
But how would I get in touch within such realm?
A person on casters who pilfers the witness, and
inculcation the lead in a pencil. Then I remember
things, like leaning up against drums the night
the blues are oaken.

Miserable news, the windows that were brought in
to open will not and the sun is out upon them.
The sentence is of durenamel but the people handle it
and do not read it. Receiving surfaces. The narwhale
cannot shake hands in the velvet corridor, which
turned to color when the rain began. Modification
Reveries, salts on sand, what continues on beyond
and below the supposedly stopped passage, my hand in
yours in the land lacking mysteries of friction and fiction.
We could go out doors and open a pencil. Did you
save the peaches for continuance in the outer realms.
We have reached thursday, what an odd fillip
of deportment. Those bored with the crystal
could exit through the nearer dormer.

Pausing to reason is it? or standpoint for
meaner statement. What could be
coldhearted in winter light? Proceeding down
a corridor in midst of open persons, the people
make of the waves a stillness with their hands.

It's possible, it's just not responsible. I'll
never learn right to write. I cross my t's
like fenceboard treeposts in a sky of wires,
or a television weary of the Christ image.
Nobody knows as far as I can see. The rest
is up as far as fire in the alphabet
of glance. The rest just her bubble as witness
of the universe going blind in going on.

•

The man walked out, but what locked in the
description of the room behind him?
His very passage was leaning in that direction, the indication
of plain speech and ordinary objects. Pluperfect
things, the ones no longer open to any eyes?
The man speaks out in the street about light.
But light from the window is a barricade.
A once noticed stanchion is rested and flows,
becomes parts of other things it had no part in
when the eyes. He had not noticed himself
even enough to say, I am leaving you.
The very door his party to disaster, or an opening out
of all roads. Streets lit and not so.
As things are dramatic *and* heedless.

•

A crystal the cold of collected standpoints.
When the time will shift down
and spell whole into points of obstructing light.
This is the universe, a solid.
An is without precedent.
A Nothing Gone.

•

"the main of things, the mind"

•

He walks down and is it said?
He walks from the door and is it spoken?
But is it, the stone in his path, to be learned in breath?
or rocked on its hinges in a saturday leaning?

The sun has turned out
the moon turned through
aisleways of thorn thought
relinquishing rolls of nerve and stupid
the curved stone, the bent cue

He walks in shortness
of stick of fieldfloat of label
and stills the hands of those who would read
the sign there stalks in time
of viable and restless and limit
a road plain beyond parse or hitching gesture
a grown thing itched up of mintless midway
an arcing count of filament dire

Fraught things glass in brain's lair
no matter an ocean of sameway caring
a stare of the free lumps at fortune's hap
a trunk hauled loath beneath capless day

Thing hath no rate
he would not dare
but the hill sheds upward
its gnash of pebble batter
its sunward and moonward

of going out and going in
all to tend the blooming
but no one to bear the stem

•

A headache in the light. And no more than
that apparent. Linings of the linger with
ague of fold. Argument to stagger on
in lips and in the place of whole trees. Are they?
A measureless banter without song to its weight.
A listing height, and in it the tread of the lightless heart.
Heart of no known head? Traceless, the vanish
of ink-sown and cast brand. The smelter of hits,
the eye to the tree. The small to the sole. The
emitter to the glanced. Elegant smolder after
romance. Give a whisper to the brain of pain
of light. Of nothing as disposable as night after
vanish of day. The rafter of knocks apace
in gold of cold stare. The whims replaced on
the air. Better treason than reason wanting?
Face in the glass time of fading. Words all encased
a wire. A trove weed, state of clothes and
coiling mention. Better to be savage than lose sight.
Of. Clicking soft word off in ways sanguine to
toss of fade urge. Cancel as the day the night
the day. The clot. Emergent bed, soaked to
the roils in section ever briefer in mention.
The head's pain lanked stiller. The cribbage
a howler. The outtance a burl.

Look up, look it up. These fragments effaced
of lock but not of tremble. The earth a
shambles, the eye a grate. The mind a mention,

tongue a scratch. Till he lift the door
from open chasm, and rear the day all
socket of mentioning done.

Preamble, to the notch prehensile.

•

How will I fill this space
with gab to lengthen shortening fires?
Amazement a buckle,
a flash a stand.
Wisdom a shortness
in the hand a shovel
a striking of plans
with a devil and his man.
These windows a shrieking
of a litmus leaving
the storming of a sand.
That sound gone
on every ear
fleshed each eye
and the marks will winter
the boring die.

•

They come down tiny in the distance to the far edge
of the middleground eyedrop pond and riot in directions.
Then walk out across the ice to the center and apply the
circular metal detector to the surface of the ice,
you hear the clump-shock echo of their shoes.

•

What I need I will get.
But the supplies must be reduced.
These words here are already too much.
Many words stand for a vast emptiness.
The only way it may be reduced to sense?
Few words to be a hugeness of forms.
Also those words to be tiny pockets
contain the things that are enough.

●

It makes me upset, it makes me upset
best is all.

The point of it all is that everything
is important, not just

●

What is it? The men beat each other. They stomp
and hoot. They are ensnarled in a glass war, as if
with ice heavily laden. They collapse faces and
pout at fists. Huge heaving grunts. Walls
dripping, sweated burlap. This is all in the dark.
No, there is a single candle, frozen steady,
scarlet shine. How is this? The men have
collapsed, the two of them. They have forgotten.
Clothing fractured. Eyeballs solid white.
There was no reason. They had forgotten
how to spell . . .

They were darned if they were going to . . .
They produced sticks. Ruddy points.
There was a mark in the wood wall one had to
prolong the other into cleaning with his tongue.
It was hard. No one knew. The sticks

began to swat like the frozen wings of insects
clattered together. Later they would dig up and
apply moss to each other's beating tongues.

They became transparent and could see blood
rolling down the inside walls of their torsos.
It seemed a language that held them up
for some hours.

Do I know who? No.
Steel in the hands of the migrant borrowers.

●

The men bent together into a hulk
held together with metal captions.
Their sizes in the slithering wind.
Who knew if the crystal would have brought
straightness to this mix.
I looked into it and doubted mathematics.

●

Smaller as the days get I am beginning to write.
Someday no one will be able to read the world.
The line is an assemblage of broken smaller pieces.
The size of the world does not matter.
The end of the line is at the greatest juncture.
At that point where one may say Emergency
    and mean time.
The strong grasp that it has not yet begun to flow.
My words have always been written across vast distances.
I have often not known what was in my hand.

A poet needs the one who will tell him what
   he has done.
And especially the world which will tell him nothing.
The days when glance was a mineral ore . . .

•

What could flash before one must not be left
out in the sun.
The indescribable beauty of the mind's light.
Such views are not squared, as poems are not held
to measurable boundaries. Sometimes they seem
to move too far too fast to be grasped more
than initially. Only in the instant of making?

•

     "Is nature a gigantic cat? If so who
     strokes its back?"

•

To dream that somebody said something, and probably
previously had met somebody, and came over and
put an arm on the counter. Nothing.
To dream exchanged identities, rolls of bills,
the top off the soup, fiddling around with soldiers'
weapons in midday, a fishing still on the fire.
To dream that instant movies occupied one's
daily hours, men going down elevators into mines
in blue shirts growing turquoise with carbide light,
whole cattlecars filled with silver change, beacons
occulting in fog swaths of the furthest sandspit.
To dream perhaps to sleep.

I think of myself later, I say to myself again.
I'll walk, *then* try the door.

●

Providing you thought of it first, it'll never have to
go away and return to surprise you.
Pain's that alarm bell, the woods will swell.

●

How much of poetry is unprovoked thought?

●

The crystal almost invisible in taking on and in
the tones of everything else in the room dominates the room.
A scatter dance held rigid, knowledge is that?
Take on the coloration and not be swerved,
chameleon? Why does all this going to be
tight and fast twirl? The desire for centers again
so outside center, offcenter to drag me
but I'm the one thought it off my mark?
Still out there, the crystal lurks without shift.
A raising of the arm over this parallel battle.

Shot of windows dividing out of phase, this route
of raised erasures, knowledge is a blend in one spot
if not a fudge. Brings you back to morning
the crystal is leaning, a learning once the arm
is removed? There is no overview but in
the local strictly system, protean as might be wished
or avoided. In, within, withheld, apparence
owns a shifty lock? Back to the thought, the crystal
open while closed.

●

Distracted by the animals and living among crystals . . .
Twining around the voice gives out . . .
I am but have not found my spot.
Ear living in cleavage of wheat remnant
clear hearing caught on the lozenge of a calcite
as if dissolved on the tongue at movie showing
the one who ingests and will never speak again.

The thought mode joint-controlled
system of narrow high hallways pinching out at the top
where the ceiling a crack and the mind arrowing, according
millions of sideways along pestiferous strata
to bank on, cake up, to surmount from within inwards
diamonds that flow even
   over warming opal batholith
   and excite the pointings
   from everywhere soaking *in*
Lights are in
perfect darkness
perfect axes
touch.

      •

The Great Meditation on Being could be the axis
of the motor fused into tree trunk by tornado
that stepped by. And the sentence the ordering.

Tugging at the thing. Didn't leave off
me. All the leaves are solvent, don't they
drop?

      •

The floor is strong stone
and you're going to smell the smoke of hard slump
when your brain goes out.

•

Invention of names
that have catalytic spines
narrowing gaps
and interest churns

Whole world a raised finger
a verb a raised finger,
an eyebrow, a full stare

•

Breaking the bright colors out in the sundown
increasing hits to the far side of dwindle
the dynamite has been licked for the last time.

•

To start out and want to be a writer . . . I didn't
want to be, I wanted to investigate and hold
the discoveries in my hand. I wanted to see
things until their names appeared and led.
It didn't seem that it would amount to a
paper life.

•

It fascinates me now to see if I find things to
speak what shapes their sentences will take.

•

The granite lid with the paper lock

•

What are they down there in their cars go by, should
I go into roadhouses and grow fat teeth?
or apply ear to phonepoles and feel wires
singe the starbreeze? Is it tantamount
to any more bucket than My Romance?
or opening up any more finally is
than giving up totally no more pen?
Go on, say what you whim.
It's gullible I suppose and the leaves do blow down
in the wet blast toward Novembers of the
blinded mind by heart torn on bender
blender and start. You know how these all
roll on as fool's days, parked millennium
prone market. The park benches matted
prove a tinder, I could wind further?
Opening of size beyond any fender my
missing blues.

•

If only what I say
could be pebble held
a strong stone of mention
no matter the hurled air
a weld caught
on fierce breath
a standing to point
of no motion

The things of world stay
around nothing or the converse
rush not away
with your fired words

The lamp a lump
or patterned daughter
brought to water and stored

•

The Balk of Everything. DeKooning in the dream
in which he is going to be on television
but by then I will be his friend
in the adventure together of the Square of Hats
where we looked up and fell down
turning to recover
the memory of the dream

and its weather the people
who lagged behind and spotted us
rolling in the electric filth
the impossibility of being anything but
confusing everybody

that the storm would come from the ball of the peak
the image of the bowl to be perfectly finished
a handout in the well of the dream
the hell of the wrongly inhabited apparel court

It was apparent, when it was not
we tumbled in the self stroked fire
were involved in silly, and observed
it all comes down
to the witness knob we'd nerved
the world, it is off now, the box
and contained the shatter

•

What is seen is what contained
in angles of the light
the type of dream in day
hours pent up and bound for blur
reflection and the intermittence of sides
striation
is where your hand has been
in stroke, in act

It lands the table
provokes the field
and in staying the hand
rattles the dream

Glowing toward the bottom into peach
a row of lamps at the sheaf of the ship
would razor off your cognizance
a slight of store
or stow the ignorance of wheat

The row of windows, remember the march
that led you to the latch
the wheat lamp's touch

•

Adequacy often enough Doubt
aqua after sufficient tilt
. . . the rays of sunshelf through nightdust . . .
Blossoms of not one shake of future
to the born, the eye, the finish
(vision's neuter)

•

Paper scarcer, poems more meant
to the shorter end
I want the lines to dive, delude

In density is destiny mixed

●

A cut of light
                or a cutting
grows of a whole night composed
of day as well
the day the crystal's axes in a swarm drill
preciseness bristles of an emptiness sure
caught to tongue and left to lip
imitant blur
a night caught in such angles lit

●

One could divide it all up into
those who know how the work should be
and those who never know before the work.
But then those who did not know began to know
the materials, an intimate action
and can one go too far with material causes?
(will and would
    rather than
 shall and should)

●

Roars in the Heavens
are nodules of the apple
throat to commit leaves

the whore's decimal, void apparel
a plant, a wind whim
you'd cancel what you didn't hear

●

I am become so sensitive to sounds. The least
knock puts me off my pitch. I want to
hear the slightest curve of the tongue.
                    (kitchen clatter over Lear)
Am I bound to be a sender, not a receiver?

●

This place where morning is permanent
what do we have for coffee in this doorway breakfast
a milk-sugar reduction of haulable hulls?
No spots that are not stuck shadows on collected grounds
no legs that are larger than their permanent laundries.
Can this be salvation, bunker with a petaled ceiling
and no battery lights, no wheat lamps?
I am arrangeable but the day features no last laps
no solution firmer than a cap for your pet
laggard in formation, cat that hired its mice.

●

What if the light shard remained
on the floor after the sun had passed on?

●

Should I really have to know
what kind of sentence I like?
Writing is like speaking while
not speaking and what can I see

of that speaking while not?
Not much. (image of lips closing quickly
                        and perhaps forever)
"What kind of writing do you do?"
(this kind of person has not even a glimpse)
Now what do I think I have created? Solitude.
                        (remains to be seen)
And if I am afraid, then what? Spin the crystal.

•

I am not to speak for one year.
The arm is out of place and the window too near the face.
It might be tender but it has no handle.
The golden brass of the standard fear folds
wherever its breaded catch is known.
Behind the barn a leaflet chides discovery unbound.
Unfounded all such chastisement. A bold
and clicking facade. A roam to its frame.

I am not to pretend myself out of wine or wind.
The sleeping vine with cat, or yellow band around the oak.
Shown shards of blue open in twig space, in loft
or sprint of glance. I am not open nor am I in
close. The cabinet to contain the bones of the one
who would wish, who did stand and will tip
where no gem but something rushes,
a thing stretches.

I am to reach and thin, not perch.
An immaculate back in a certain knock of torsion.
The screen of a filament tans an appearance of motion.
A lock on the wind, a mind released, in the main.
On the strand, a flick of the hand, an assertion
that makes not an odd of the flame in sand,

a sound and beyond it nothing, not one shade of flinch
over bolt and over lodge, the egg is not large
and stays.

•

Vast toy tower, erector set crossed rods, aloft in the
winds it bends, box of instruments padlocked
attached high up, wires locked and stretched, guy wires
over whole field countries of bramble and fir, almost
winter I hang and reach out over, hills to the terminant,
propeller at the very ice tip of the mock tower, this
its land and this the cemented end.

We grow and we loose ourselves. An arch over
wary turntable land, autumn grit so parsed
it enables, and the wires stretch and thong in the
wind. I am amok in the height
and cancel over all a blue screen and unblink day
and surface the rats that hoard remnants of
meteor instrument below ice pack below
stir ground, below and above, below and encasing
treatment. I howl and the world staves its
nerves. I will make concert of the wings
the clouds have clattered. No more sundial
face to the whole of it. Truly face.
Rust rock bench. World terminus, skinny
tower. Worth nothing, worth of nothing serving.
Terminant tip. To which all rolls beckoning.
An earth of pure shield, a sky ice dry.
And sound as a fire the sound of a wire,
no one or thing remain to the touch.

Tip of locked belts over Rat Battle Land.

•

The crystal is always showing a world
that does not exist except in remission.
It does not contain but transposes.

The whole point of this
house is to change the light.
No one is to live there in fact
its precise location is not known.
Everything goes on around it
changes within it, beyond help
beyond hope beyond the very name of heart.
Yes, the crystal is a house
one is inhabited by.

I crystallized myself out of flesh
but this is wrong. I learned to scratch
down words on paper by tendency of crystal
adjacent to sleeping area. When I was home.
When I was even a noun.

(The monkeys want in here but I parry them)
The books are arranged shelf
by crystal shelf. The numbers I have given them
give me sleep. An age at which
I replaced the crystals with printed words.
Now I am come of age.
Now I can no longer lie.

Infinity exists, therefore impossibility does.
                    (Q.E.D.)
An antipython spelling its life through miles
of dusting page. Searching through aisles
of collapsing volume for the spine of a single creature.
It lives near the square of the concrete church and
this is its address: Forgotten Routes.
I sat on a chair there and waited for

the papers to near.
In that basement would be
rubber waves and chocolate volumes.
In that air would come
worth and stress.
The woman would reject no clothing.
She herself in a form of remission.
My hand is on the stair though I am
comfortably seated. My only fear
that I will not forget.
The crystal to remember.

Chocolate cake, rubber wands, calypso in plaster,
a static emitter, a length of butter, the stage
in darkness, a crumpled-up tongue mess, Blake's
compass, the golden rectangle, body by Fisher,
a Balthus land letter, all my tomorrows in a
single vein of sand, or sound, or stilled light.
Better you reach out and grasp it and touch it to
your mask.
It coils your days to a certain same.

•

Where is the wonder to not know?
It's an apparent of life, to take as apparent.
Visions seen, heard, felt, dropped for another,
repasted in a new cover, thought up and then
sent down again, traipsed for and wished
and then to see them snap back to sender but
not see the sender, I have grateful needs.
The words say. Nothing today is apparent,
just there, nowhere, bent over the task,
removal of the mask, the tendency to bow
and tend, kneel at the feet of the statue
of whole stone, white caps, inverted needs,

no one knows, no one knows better than to.
The path follows and portions weed lots and
the former goddess statues.
We See, is not allowed. But a frightening fan of
the forms beneath the curtain. I take a breath,
I style it. I am interminable at the dead
crystal that will never turn off. I laugh
and spin it. I did not laugh just then
as it hoops a shadow on the bright wood. Bright word.
Knuckle over the loops of what steadies to be said.
Sure to write all this down here, sure and doubt.
The crystal seems filled to slant line of terminus
but is itself a filling of all now empty whole.
Things holes in things, lights in stops, breathing
within hearing. A bath in blood, a hood over
the normal watcher, sipper at form's blade.

And where is the known wonder?
The seven, of which memory leaves vacant one,
or two. I take off its shoe and it
breathe on you. Who are me a hundred million
careless and sieved-off times or wavelets or
forks from the shine. You are me, I am
sure interminable. You, crystal, it and forgotten.
High and far and tiny on my bureau of born sheaf
and short regret. The knowing of which is interminable,
though as wonder short. A cry in the wood
that bends the limbs. A sheep in a frame
for later commission.

Sleek friendless tendencies.
Shock in reach of coldness at fingertip.
Calcium rates silicon, socket to terminal.
I put on the hat as a bow to truncation.
Linear life times five, times seven, times turn
at all, onlooker. The hats were beveled cones.

The nights were seeded in doubts, level fires,
coarse pocketed finds. The lock became the kicker.
The light a stone.

A kind of time. An implacable placement in
felt time diminish. Dots on a paper
of silk to decipher, waving tongs over a net
to seal the stars. Our fates are to motion
as sand is to shoe. Sound as a cap.
The termination is many, the directions of many.
The telephone will not ring in this seal of light.
This one pent of night. This stone, I throw you
away but you return. You have returned this shine.
You have spelled my shoe in a minute of melody, a
day far away now in horizons of leather.
The scroll not to bother. The ancient as a sever
as here today as any stone. My uncle put up
on a ranch his aerial in sand, but such is lie.
So I shift. I dream of putting my shirt over
the crystal to little help. And watch it that
the temperature settle. The words give me battle
in even rows and warm. And warn of war
at the homestead hearth, valve of the heart,
ear that won't start if the crystal rattle.
Not so, but once it bubbled.

Ancient as a spine, motor to whisper in the
wafter region. A Realm, zone of stood stone,
carved breath before a face could result. Or a
zircon in basement. Cold cereal on Xmas bulbs
in the room below Halloween. The pictures so
slow to frame, the crystal seen turning. Space
to colden the breath, husk of an anciency.
I walked out over the books, the street was so plain.

Vodka as standard, Tequila in a topaz
is what makes it yellow. The worm left out.
Slats and rulers the room warms, the time is coming up.
It will be left, you and I, to us only to turn.
You crystal, you lock my way. Lurking and looking
for familiars to play. The melody is firm
in the crystal of temper, little or no dot to enter.
As the freedom has withered, so goes the heat for your fate.
I mumbled and scattered, I would not sit for
what I knew. An empty light the cue.

For whatever you can't know you do write.
Sleeping stalk through the night, witless curvature.
Some anagrams of the Mock Crystal. Snail shell
of rust in the dream window. Humid practice
of the vermiform ways. Balanced on the skull
in a bed of potatoes. Hands never to
exit the sleeves and the camera still clicking.
Eyeholes in the seamless places. Going home
a matter of form as everyone has gone and done.
The nose, the petals of zinc, the goat at a door.
The liquid for which there is no rest or shiftless spot.
Dreams in which gardenias start and hop.
My own face lies without a trace.
And I write them with the greatest of wills to know
and so do not.

Let's stop. The crystal still spinning. Nothing to know yet
has a bearing. Withal apparent in such of a light
it should be ringing. My ankles should be humming.
And my eyes start turning. I lift my fire where
my hand should be, cool as caliper at the
rusty wood. Cancel, says the epigram,
cancel and begin. Start ash to confer upon

the light a breed. Standard of fright in
the crystal's place, in the crystal's stead
a match for the eyes.

•

The moon comes into the ceiling. Everybody who
comes to know there comes to know that.
But the crystal is stolid. Only to write only
thinking in the cracks. To think is not to put
anything down. It all goes the same way
off soft in a line. A line of pearl
handles, nothing to do with the crystal. And
it is not made of petals to be thinking of here. Further on
it will be cancelled, what grows. That it has
grown, that and only. Bending over the crystal
they all wondered what writing would proceed.
Would it all be of crystal an apparency. Nobody
has thought, the way the crystal takes apparent root.
If only speech could talk. If only talk could
grind down beneath willful feet. The crystal
was out of favor, out of any such space and time.
For talking would not root it, condescending not
spill it out. A whole volume of thought
spun out for naught, spelled out as well
as a tooth might be brushed, a tooth no longer
well dwelt in the head. As stolid as a jaw
might be missed, this crystal. The earth
moved them and I thought, a further oddness, further address.
Thought is always further, of a furtherance down
the chiseled line.

All this is too lean. Water never lean,
the crystal has me think of. As my marks do.
As any such leavening would turn my crystal fear.
But such is not mine. Possession of a crystal

would not enter. Or a crystal processional
as if entering a city. The gates were of a stone,
plain and bore no thought. Or if so, passed through
limber and forgotten. But my writing is uneven.
And it is not even morning. The moon is in
the ceiling. And the crystal on the board.

And going in all the while I was livid with fear
but a crystal would ease my care. I put down
the numbers, six, for the common crystal.
Numbers can not be thought about, but a crystal
can take on mind. Make you the surrounding
subject to, the subject always surrounds. And I
will never make clear my grounds. Never well make
it would be. The sides of life that are even ones.
Integers then to hold a transparency. Buildings
to surround them and take other life in them.
The hold of light. That the moon says small
part of this. That the moon says, how little do
we hear. If only little body, the planet on
the table. It fancies a marry of water and
shock. Still, the crystal takes up zero, a
center tween my eyes. My health and subsequent
lies.

The character had written his poems, the lineaments
of crystal. The character past. Whether he
was glad at that or he wished at all, that
will be subject to diminishment the crystal protects.
All go away with the poems, all go right away, out.
Finish, proceed, dote on failings bright, hover
in the sheavings of the semblances of night.
An evenness of crowings as the dawn begins.
Begins to strew again, fixed begins that scatter
the rising rest. The mother in no nest.
Next. Trust. Apparency is gaining on the

grounding of all fibers, even optical if.
Even bounded face. Such as regular facets
to the masking of water. The bright whole
of the table's gem.

If I could stand up hollowly in the crystal's speech.
The breathener's reach. Ringing globe,
saddled with pens. Glow ball envy of ropes.
End product shine of all stallings. It is not a
gem but true poise of water standing.
As if whole volume of make-work gave a daughter.
A better. Remained after the slaughter standing
like no pen. My eyes again watch and nothing
is parallel. No one is wondering and the earth
is clear. End point. Pendulum near.

•

It's sharp enough to tempt water.
The portions of a substance, how fast?
The eliminations, subsequent, of space,
of the locks on a charm, of the sea's waters,
the portions invisible from any land or standpoint,
how ritual, how divisible, how plain a calm?
A reaching of the hand to a handle, a
more's the reason to shine when invisible.
And the cuts of light, how little a strain.
On hand, on boards, on a night without moon.
When far off the points of a storm have landed.
Where I am careful before the stone.

The crystal is bent, but encounters no salvage.
A crock of misty appears, a lock of standages
pryly averaging, so I will savage it. It knocks me.
I answer it, with a wristy itched smear, log all
stretch of land to a hole for a year

and sing its inches down. Pretend you won't loan
yourself and *are* a crystal. The walls don't stand it.
It turns to the left of light. The sanity of
brittleness will not save you, its stare.
Locks, it says something about, locks that set
not a piece together. The holes it frequents have none.
Stop thinking to write. Go to sleep and let it hold.

•

Anti-vacuum. Anti-thoughtfulness.
Random reflections? Fractures encased.
The thing wants nothing, wants for nothing.
I'll take a glimpse, a long stare, the look
that brings semi-wakefulness. A blue flake
from the sky and how does it arrive in there?
What am I looking at. Into what's locked businesses?
Perfectly, or is it, then clear? Standing gear.
I could ink it all closed? Like what in there?
Fractions of the outer, shuffled and contained.
Make up a list and remain without. Stop.
Lift your weapons. Here is the one that resists intentions.

•

For that matter, why know any mineral?
Sometimes I'd rather knowledge were the pleasure
of taking any book down off a high shelf, the long
arm reaching of that leverage.
The thing is also a light, some say. More even the reverse.
The object of scrutiny. A phrase is also a wave.
Carved to see better. Looking at angles not designed by men.
For that matter the race leaves no direction but
follows them all. That nothing may be left to stand.

I let it go in all directions here. Mayday from boredom,
shine on the pall.
We've not always got to see you think you crystal.

•

They've known about all this sharp stuff nearly forever.
Nights when the blade was made, days when the drinking glass.
Nero had two goblets carved at great expense with
Homeric legend and then smashed both in a rage.
Crusaders from the stuff got grail ideas and rode
rusting off. Stuff perhaps the wrong idea, but
crystal itself does fill. Then it does not need a word.
In the caves the clear weight was enough. They saw.
The one word of unknown origin.

The crystal does not provide. It subsists.
But what I know
is not its point, certainly not, pendulum weight.
Light as it is not in hand, a tryer though I am.
Perhaps it wanted to be all different ways and
isotropically came out this? Loaf enough I'll see?
During, see during, see the end of the line always receding.
As some thing that does not need needing, a tremble.
A hollow thing is not a standard. Weighted
toward which end will now this . . . ?
All of this nothing toward a single scent.
One mile before the daylight that never . . .
One sign left in a jacketed glow
one thought that I could not
even try to sift.

Rest of the morning spent in curving
while this what of it stands. It points

to the level of day I will light. I will hand
over to the hurling wind, division of solace,
plaque of friend.   (American Whisper Band)

●

Everything that surrounds
it and is not
part of it

●

The way time feels on metal, I love its ride.
Sober sticking on the outside, points, striking points
that ride on a sheet of air above the plate base.
Knowing here does not aid but could lapse you
sheer away. The way time is made, absently
in perfect focus, riveted eyes, crystal hand,
thought off yourself to rise in this work.

●

Morning to frighten. The yard's trunks
to be candles awaiting lightning.
But I dismiss this early Fall Boston of lines
the better to hold lying better than thought.

●

Sides of the world, throbbings of the sound axes.
Writing on the side of a page, a wall
in a world of inter-bladed and filtering walls.
They do not revolve, exactly. They intertwine,
jolt across segments, planless. Lives are
an unsynchronized result, a night without
metal tongs for hands, thoughts that hover

winds over beach, straight face, stained waters.
I have never had any bother with brothers.
But now perhaps sisters are gaining on me?
If the metal had been heated what would its
surfaces say. I lined myself
according to you who are you? Granted the night,
granted the lifted blades of day. Cry them not
and heat that the light. I can write anything if
I switch forms by hand. I can make
the window listen?

Then is the crystal striking.

•

A cancer filled up with water. A stretch
in the pod bay. You do not have to know what
went over on my back. I opened the transom,
sweaters. Loops of oil. Flasks with initials.
Thirteen dots in a major realm. I thought I told you
what I couldn't even imagine. Just in truth.
Blood on the sleeve. Intentional armistice after
bargaining session. They all had plans for it not
brought out before. Animal lessons. Discursive
and folderol mention. Drive the stork through
the window shield. Imagine characters
pretending to stay. And loop over the frigidaire
of the blue sky. The card says stung, and that's
the bottom of it. Size. Perfume.
Interregnum bargainers in lemon get-up stationing.
I've got to use these words. Use them up?
Stand down from such of them? Nothing further
to erase blindness. Superficial node, self-canceling.
She comes in the door and worries about warped fruits.

I say the cat knows me, and she leaves by the
same door. The opening of all things, clapboards
to reveal the divided loot. No one there had
known to look. Windows to keep going by
and up and down. We humans are listeners but
we can't keep our mouths in synch. Alarming
and willing the neighbors to stay up and give notice.
Start and then lapse back, the airs one hears between.
Today everything kept coming back wrong.
A subtle knock at the base of the brain.
Barring dreams of candy razors.
Tonight the sun was all over the kills, in Dutch
with creeks. Take all my letters away, I
don't want them here. That I may sit up
with my fear. But diaries too are dialogues
and here I only grasp one end. Tantamount
to jealousy of the void.

·

There's fish in the bottom. And breakfast flakes,
and sun shard. It clouds and unclouds itself.
So does my handwriting. But it always stands,
as my brain it is standing there. Perch
hanging slightly above the bottom. Iron crackle,
sticks in your gloves as you're stripping the machine
for painting. And sun makes a loop of a shadow.
Gold bars of beveled light enclosed. I piss
off the porch and the moon shines how gold my
strand in the air. Night air tends strange facets.
Hear me, crystal, shake me loose.

Yeah, I've been over there a few times and I don't
want to talk about it. Listen to me, it's best
you get it out. Will be on your stomach
as if a brain would float.

All along the highway there are dips in the temperature.
Freezers linked to logs while all else suns.
Tankers attached to flags, whore mumbles
in exoneration momentum. Bulks
on the fly, and insectiferous the edges to cloud.
I sit down no trumps and catch a whiff-heft
of the long gone by talks. And so splenderous
the empty, the haul on color toning, the
novembers pending.

                            •

Slot talk. A certain tone, whatever. I have
my worries and I have my names. Sometimes all
the words. Could you say, What's his word?
The word of whom? Do they all jam toward voice?
Toward question? All writing a call in
darkness: Word?

Stop the shop talk. What if you only had an hour
to live? Too little time to think more than
about how there was only a little more time.
Is it always the middle of the night when you think
about time ending? What is the exact mid-point
of the darkness? This time of year (November)
it must be nearly midnight. But I always think it
2 or 4 in the morning. I remember mornings
when I saw the sun come up, the first false dawn
glow then the full thing, over a green bedstead.
And others in my father's room, in bed with
Fred, Long John's Party Line just going off the
air at 5:30 with those slow Manhattan strings
and crystal dew-air celeste notes ringing and clinging
and wafting, hot sun in the cool air of summer
dawn coming up over the Bullock hedges and
backyard trees across the street. Fine feeling.
Early in life all over again and whatever you had
to do today was new.

Going over tales of flying saucers in the
sunrise. Everything everybody could have thought
to say said. Morning, go to sleep.
A prime point. The sun is an unmarked
flying celeste . . .

Me alone, I wonder if I have any
true idea who. Certainly not an image.
But something else one could write?
I'll never actually recognize it but it's all
in here somewhere? By-product of
the writing addiction?

The crystal seems to contain tiny wire snips.
Catching the light. Throwing the tiny messages
itself can't use? Kerouac stares at me
from the yellow button.
Tell it well and truly, Go moan for man, etc.
Writing noises in the night instead.
Scratching minutes. Companion apparel of
the long sentence.

•

The crystal lies. Its sides are unequal to me.
Sheers me in mind of chronic weights.
Its imaginations of bare state. What could
one say?, crystal dimming on the horizon.
Sensational an increment, tiny, over-
apprehended and crazed. I do not fit to it,
I dial it and spin it, head on in phases.

I haven't got the least idea, I don't know, it
doesn't really seem, perhaps after all, when,
but all notions could add up to nothing but.
I haven't got it, I can't see it, it does nothing

but blend, smear, toddle a bit to the sides,
make a mask of its initial, there can't
after all be a conclusion to ideas?
Sensations finish? Descriptions stop?
Images impede the flow?
A leading question, a leading image?
The crystal spots itself. My imagination narrowed
to a tiny rock in a room.
And my throat so dry at the thought.

●

Small place. Invasions of Small Place.
Rock on a board. But not rock it's
mineral organicism. The word mineral
gives organic touch to the flow. Flow, hell!
Immovable neck of the world. Mineral
notching of pristine sense, self, an interior *gone*
floating in the patched wall. And beyond, nothing
beyond. Monk strike key, and all presumed
depth to shoot out later? He likes
the sound in the room, nothing now to be
patched. Ring. Ring be the mineral
quotient of blocks to move?
Scratch. Wobble. Ring got no fear.
And all around mumbles to the flock of
crystal nub. He spots the center of world
with thumb. And not to be caught out
in shame and blame of name. Writing
could be like striking thing. Thumb it
into metals at the centrum of time.
Time's square stair/stare of squeak cheer
and milder chair. Trees rock to my knees.
And preposterous, this fault block of any man
in room. I divided myself here
and left the ceiling ringing.

No story. I can't discipline myself to follow the
single thread. There is no single road
leading off. A road does not just start
but it does lead. How it leads, all over,
never finished. And I strictly see
all the sides, what the tangents are pursuing me,
consuming me, with. With as a halt on
progress? We are battered by chromaticism.

Open the mind to everything, and then follow the ink.
One suitable phrase leaves no hope. Leave
the tongue out! That it catch, while no
longer allowing speech? Everything seems it
could be question or exclamation. Wondering
about hours, and their things. How one could
tell the seasons blind, just by the sounds of
their leaves (Kurosawa). Oldness
cannot be made up. I believe in the
seeing left for myself.

These scratches irritate. Seems I will
write anything now. I blunder on through
myself and never meet. Strictly to see it,
street and light. Walled in to the brain's studio.
Watch the ball of basis roll down over the
world's sun. Hewing it less to go home.

•

Trying to take a piss out of a hard-on, he sat,
contemplating the window of its trees.

•

They're out there in the barn juggling gumdrops
and raising a whole lot of caterwaul.
Cafeteria music, seeped in from under-the-empire
pipes. Standard elevator rhymes and whistling
pitches. Pictures of the lemon tree in scald.
Notes of people taken while they're thinking of
heaven with a grim visage. Frowns
with elephant grace-notes. Lights dancing in
the cabbage factory, where they're trapped for duration.
All those people up there in black suits taught
not to let their feet tap. It's hopeless!
In which Mozart's plumes are trapped.

●

The work of heaven or hell: to somehow
become aware of a howling in the motors.

●

A notebook full of dead-end starts.
Chiseled striations showing attempts to grow in other ways.
Change in the atmosphere overall. They did not attend
the game, which was won, which was lost anyway.
The crystal on the table while they were absent.
Light weather there or away. Light amongst
all and so
never go. Light has its poles and this is one.

●

The cigarette on the table.
The crystal on the planet.
There are blurs in this.
Thoughts that skid as well
as bind. Linkages are

not all support. Sometimes
some things just sit.
          And
then no lack of force
what?
      are blues in this
and tin sorts, wire of a tensile
strike down whole roads
dormered in sky, such openings
as we leave for the border
the holder that it is.

          •

What is seen and what is not seen. What is
molded to go. The house opened into a hillside,
green water, a sort of lemonade, clods. The boards
rattled at a cleaving in the house's hunch. It stops,
a clock, for the mentioning of bread. Little stillness
left in this whole, this barnlike settled city.
No one knows here as how anyone here knows.
Slivered in shadow, rocks at hand, milkcow lured to
the curling glen. Not to know how to empty the hen.
The crystal, and again its slight lights. A meadow
and a handle matched. The window opened onto
such a prong of sky, it hatched, then it twinned the land.
The postman opened his palm. There was a date.
There was a stretched stone. Sign of trouble, sign of
glowed statue. He had painted them blue, red,
yellow. A fear of rising brighter. The wind
allowed and scattered the helmets. A plain.
A page, on which the other books had traveled.
The time I know, and other ones also known
the crystal turned true.

          •

"The great art of films does not consist of descriptive
movement of face and body, but in the movements of
thought and soul, transmitted in a kind of intense
isolation."

•

All these things that creep into something
creep meaning there before you think
to see to meet in mind diagonal, to see
to think, blinding out to rubber of a last "to"
before the being, the own fascinating being
submerging . . .

It's lasted, now think again
it's thought, now the last thought
before now which think
to see, to have now always been
as far as
as taut as
I'm of a mind that
a mire in me makes

Lines out of mind a gasjet of sky makes
blue, blue see, blues of the roentgen kings
rent of a clogging clear tobacco lighter
blue as a hand out of conscience
wondering the rock to a stop on its table

But it's still and was before you
facing, and links the space to the blank space
facing the clear cut depth of bind
of window signed with cracks of taut growth
an avenue before you that'll spell you won't
reach up to here, a crystal waits or a near one
rise up to take thought almost

The pen is closed
the window is sticks
the crystal

•

I just lived there and never thought about it.
What was there, who were we? The plants didn't
antagonize the bricks, the cat *ate* the bugs, and we sat
on the porch after his father had died and I thought it
must be a relief, as much as convention radio has
not much to do with waiting for the fish on a beach.
It was Providence, a town, not a city really
with only one tall building with a greenish mentholated
light that should have hissed in the night even when
it wasn't raining. Still I didn't have to imagine
blimps when they all hung over that town like the
vision of a war I knew nothing about.
Brighter days when I was dim.

•

In case you see. In case you see.
I spell it. I spell it trees in the window board.
I have poem, I don't know it from Adam.
What is the first alphabet in a series? What is
a word's name? I could say I have no French,
no algebra to those moments. On the fly
parsing the dots. Cubes of life future
with holes for impression instead of circles for motion.
Go to Princeton, do not pass. Momentum
rather than fiction. Is there a half-broken-open rock?
A partially-littered table of things to be done. To be
done thought to be done thought. The thought-out things
are half-managed. Handwriting and proper spelling

in the same action? Or as in painting, the hand
prepares? I have no notion, he said and waited.
A co-rehearsed block is seen.

•

The ways in which I didn't think of it as literature.
A chair that could read. I put the words there
in those ways, excitement, doubt, in a moment
I could see it all differently. It would look
doubtful in mornings, as if written by someone else
better late nights. It took me a long time
(years) to think of myself as a person who would write
these things. Things . . . I still don't know
wholly what they are, any exact response. But I think
I always thought of myself as someone who improvises.
I didn't think of myself. I said to myself
I will make something up in a moment. Then
I will look at it, perhaps I will dispose of it
by writing something further.

I still don't easily think of myself as a writer.
I still don't think of myself. I look at the writing
and sometimes see the self in there, out there, and wonder
how I was somehow that self being written, writing
itself out as if unwinding a spool of . . .
I only see certain strands.

There are great lakes, but not in the Casbah.
The foot often slips, off what?, and I pay
out more lengths, I follow with an unrecorded eye.
The ear has no problem following. I often wonder if
it is in fact leading. It will always be the
mystery, that self end up out there as those words,
a mirror impossibly deep. Never enough words
to the bottom of the distance. Sometimes voices

that echo from nothing ever visible. If I am
asked what I am doing I look and make up
for that person.

All the words make sense. As I often do not.
To what I often hear I can hardly hold the pen.
Don't talk to me of mechanisms.
None of them work enough to please my solace.
Sometimes there is a far response and I catch a
glimpse of my death. Keep moving, I tell
that self the words have come to me to be. ·
This is all becoming a scrawl I will hardly hold
to read.

Tell someone who you are. I did it.
I did it. I did it at every point.
The private pen has inked a vast presence
in the public silence. Writing has never been as
solitary as now, I feel. I feel tense.
I feel huge.

Memory blocks me with every problem in the book.
Forgetfulness allows me to move. What do I know?
That I do not, I do not want. To know I
would have to read nothing but my own words past.
I haven't the time. I only *have* time when I
move off each mark. Don't think of,
somebody said, I am thought. The odd way
that my own past words are never things remembered.

The way thought about writing is always afterthought.
He waited behind the empty car to think of what
he might have done. The voices always passing me
until I find the way to link on and inhabit. You must
say the words until they say me, Beckett said that.

•

In which ways have I not yet thought, and the
literature in between. I have moved things around
again, dispensed and shouldered. The world is not
in any way, anyway at all. Those ways are the only
ways, always will, always doubt. I would excite
myself overly if not for the difficulty. But
it is all not difficult, it is a longer swim. A morning
with no daytime to halt it. A peek into the side of
the glassine sea.

I still don't know I thought myself to think
myself to take a look of it. Pitching of the
long time to exact repose. Picturing things, myself.
Long enough fast to a writing something further.
A leaner and an adder am I. Bewitched, bothered
and unbuilded. A twittering differing child again.
And another, a smaller hotel? And I said
to myself then: Dispose of it. Spell it back to
yourself to reenlist the charm. Improvising
is what someone took me to something to be
written by. Inverse lesson by positive adage.
Negative numberage, as if a settling bulb, as if
something I wholly didn't will. The numbers
turned up again, all the words respelled. The number
of a hill, the name of a hand.

Then I said to myself, think, but was writing
something further. The numbers all got away again,
a ceaseless cough. A marrying window, the
beachfront with the wallpaper, a smile with
the scissored crab. But I think what I said
to myself improves myself, lesson missing.
Just that which I said to myself now is missing.
The window missing, salt from the paleness of sky.
Trouble is, not that the words are missing, but just

missing. Voice taps in the top of any table,
the words for *this* table. I said this, I
said of myself think.

Stable portion, sense lesson, icicle twilight.
But that could be photo taken and not self written.
Sometimes I just don't see the door. When
the door's self is missing? I still don't see self
as opening. Who are you that what could think
of marrying.

•

The crystals in the plant.
A certain alga contains rotating selenites.
There is no use. Or if so not known.
The one on the table is not in use at present.
Or is it? Unknown and yet so present, it does
with the light what only it can. I look.
My hand stays. What is the use? I am out of service.
The crystal shines.

It says to me: Enclose the water in the hand.
It says not say. It stay.
I drink, it slant.
I wait for it to become, to fill. One day
I will walk into this room and it will have
turned opaque. It will be an uncrossable red.
It will have filled with my blood?

•

I put down words here, that they will not
share me.
Words that are shavings off the irreducible block.
Words that remain the elegance at Chaos Gate.

●

Apply the cold crystal to the cool lungs
stemming a fit of light
backwater
            left over to sod
the light goes off
to preach back of tobacco barns
(Lemuel Pitkin and the eyes of solace)
This is too even, the crystal both
even and not
evil as it is
and run out the dunking string
Hymn to Solus
chest of a tang
remnant glow in false fall
a slaty eye turned up
the fear ball lateraling

●

It's a sorrowful magic to take up this tone again
when the grey stripe of my overcoming hardly
allows me pick the words up to pitch.
There is a ceiling and it is not easing,
that rafters me back, collapsed in
calypso of eclipses, the red sphere tongued
through the shunned background.
Ready. Ready should have a collar
or color of the perfect die.

●

Dark story. Litter entry.
Literal service and fending score.
Don't want to know, not less than do.
And stand, stand over, stand up
for the trees to tie my maps.
The shore is anywhere, last place
the book ends.

●

Scan this:
                Hello, you don't know me, you have friends.
Time is not possible, a ford of nerveless rivers,
white collars shorn from weather map. Major
ones, really incredible but not nearly stood,
sidepoint avenue in the druther weathers. Initials
called off the inside of the soda bottle, self defense.
Dotted lines down the hands and bled pants. Sports
are knowledgeable, clouds blown away from north of
origin. Orange peach at liberty in attendance,
logged on the backs of terror puns. And then the offers
to reeling aislers. A lot of people are reading
what about you. Some more ball stuff.
Filings of words jumping all over tongues. However settled
can a sender be. I bought a truck on the way home
from a general delivery. I knew no tree until
too late. No comment from the bandaged side.
And baste the coats three-sides, we'll do better by
the strolling eaters. Weather has not changed much,
blueprint coldtype. With me later, the Heller
in Pink Tights.

How do we cope with when do we go back from?
Where am I on now? The insidious nature of
listening to too much music. Don't know, not
visibly sane. Think they can have an attitude

toward too much pollution? Hearing the footsteps
at the creaking door, hood, decimals amounting
to the grey coat. People do have the tendency
to think. But most of my growing up was
done sick. What I was interested in is
that here you are. You tend to personalize
it, the box, in here. Basic book distancing
theory. These processes, these sufficiently
multiple characters. Grand view subverse hotel.
Flailing the broken diction of a sunken TV. Terribly
sad but a great big fat fact. We'll be thinking
too fast, we'll be taking your sweater.

                                        : radio.

●

What is knowledge, where is the expedient?
Down what gradient, or up same? Do you know
these words' names?
I have not seen you lately, I rust on the grade.
All the things I could speak of if I had the handles.
All the present force of moving spaces. One further
to the left, and another one left to further. There is no
point from which, only the point from which you.

●

She turns the corner, sees no one, keeps going,
waits, full face, empty doorway, enters,
walks, turns to see, nothing, down the hallway,
ends, two ways to look, no one, turn
right, a longer hallway, pictures, turning, stops
in the empty, full face, not a one, starts
again, along, narrows, comes up on, taps,
full face, the wrong one, apology, backs a step,
turns, looking, empty doorway, empty hallway,

walks without notice, blank, dead wall,
turns, a last entry, not going, not noticing,
no one, not a chance, emptiness, full face.

Did you notice my face that time?

•

Interest in structure only in the terms that a
language exists. Exists and or languages,
entrances and exits. The world you have
left from telling you going on exactly wherein.
The words continue, to reconnoiter the echo.
And this ersatz follower, you.

He signified that there was always something out there,
always also not in here. With them, all time,
all things, voices saying it and saying again it does,
it has, it will. It has will, said so once,
says so more and further, it was merely wanted
and never appears. So. Lone follower of you.

The brick wall, the grey kiln. The rose and the
specialty letters. You'll never know it green as
its width would. Started again, and then
loss of memory, stop. Entrance to the
focal, the vocal fold blocked. Continue anyway
as does a pocket redness and intermittent speech.
The one beside you, no one beside you, has the language.

•

They had wanted to go over there and see those people
but the car kept moving. Poles went by.
Streams, and blown paper listing in air at odd angles.
I looked at my companions. I didn't like them.

They were too perturbed in ordinariness. Slavish
revulsion, putting caps back on pens. There was always
a window to look out from.

He makes it back to the base and only then discovers
that night has fallen. The barracks is ink.
Moldering sounds. What could have kept anyone
from standing himself lay around at every hand.
Give me the pliers.

So he looked into it. And found out nothing.
He had tried it out, came up empty. Investigation
of a fraud was itself one. Leaving early only to
leave it late. Tiny copper bells attached to the
evergreen trees in the plaza. Late light, always,
if only sometimes morning late. So he had looked.

I turned on the radio, static. A kind of
muscular bell shoving aside all other signals and
leaving its traces in mystery shows, telephone
exchanges, musical snatches. Radio should come
with a hood like a car.

I thought it would be possible to stay here, but
now I find the only possibility is not to leave.
Follow that either which way and understand it
potentially. The words under the rules are
irons on the sink, draining constantly into an
imprimatur you never actually understood.
It was given to me later, I never quite required,
to think of it more quickly each time. I have
the thought to stay here but not ever to think here.
Leavings are all you'll have asked for. I think
it will be staying here that might move me forward.

Abysmal creation, he thought and stood up.
The gradual collapse of handwriting through the ages
as a possible point at issue. There was nothing
definitely there. Everyone stood up and, tiring,
went on.

Bad thoughts behind the car. He had made it back
to the Radio House. Usefulness. Crash belt shadows.
Elemental sandwiches. Hard habit to be brief.

●

The crystals are cogs in something.
One cog
that balances away from birth
this one
that silences me

●

Directionless roads, all of them. At once I
stopped to think of it in just that way.
One might become stalled, thinking in too large
a containment and threaded every through and which way,
attracted at a loss. So huge, and yet a not
uncommon complexity. As if looking down at a
shoe, a stand of wheat there. As if the pen
led an unfathomable hand writing.

It's all sensible, all so meaningful. Thus
unfollowable, the limitless cogency. Start with
something. Begin here. No matter how balled-up
you become, leaping past averages the gathering
wisdom, gathering into leaded hulk. Stop
to think? Thought never ceasing, erasing.
Certainly, the hard momentum of forgettal.

I go past places I never thought, and some I did.
Some link up without my stopping to. Most
never do. Hole in the night for a pendulum,
missing. The stroke swings past the
building edge into a far crevice no one has seen
the paper of, the color of that eye. Clock on
the corner strikes itself dumb. Learning makes out
that I might benefit from the least thing here.

•

Do you prefer standing objects?
Moveless, that you can stare at
in no danger of the distortions produced by motion.
Throw the book and have done with it.
Ink in all the interims. Memorize the window's
view. Never leave yourself open to . . .

The landscape vanished, replaced by an artful ease
of man-produced objects. Candlestick,
pewter, no additional distinguishing feature.
Box of matches, sliding-drawer style, some of the
sticks with white tips some with black.
A hole in the . . .

It was lighter out today. Featureless dismals
for your pleasure. Keep the head down and
kick leaves. Exit the store by turning right,
paperbag in right hand, leading off with
right foot. Circular thinking enforced by
standard memory blocks. What is the name of
that druggist who lives behind the farm near
Newtown? And could he be the one who
mentioned being hungry for stopsigns?

•

The music levers into brain, insists
I listen to it. That I have no other
life I am a listener. (Am I lighter?)
He plays an old text, he
does it. He plays on
a text otherwise lifeless. The pressures
of his hands become my voice nodes,
stepping off the inner gradients to a varying density.
I bent my lower lip just now.
The stanzas are of gold or brass
or a folded glass shocked full of bright
outer data. Silly words, give up your
completions. The music will not spill.
It is incapable of other than his hands.

Speed is a grin or a sort of frown.
Eroticism possible with a machine? Stick
your dick in a hole and drop in your cent.
Machine a matter of waiting. Dropping the
fingers at speed into the precise rites of air,
and whistling across them too as if across metal
with the inflection of a th.

Is the solution acidic enough to stir into
a solid? Part fun part rain part
dollar bill in hand? Where is the mention
of anything such as this could be.

Martians having not a thing to do with it.
Uncapping and capping the pen having lots.

•

We go. We go there. We go there now.
There is no right place to start from.
Off from the edge of a land to the midst

of another. What is the name of
your weather, the sprawl of your language hand?
I counter with midsts, tend to that, while
sent in poise at edge, this edge.
To that, where no hand will aid.

Another America, reverse face?
A force of ape, with glass typed up as hair,
with drills will send you scrammed to basis.
Night of tendency lights, ringed but curveless.
I palm your necklace.

As electricity is homeless. Continental baseless.
Bones to a radiant inner. Coaxless stocking
the brittle tone, sash of stone without a cord.
You leave me out in weathers, the languages,
the footless mounts. Peace at table with revolver
and glass of eye in solution. There is nothing
to take but shocking, the syrupy time of its length.
The sun on a gesture, a culture, a nodding a shaking, and
I drain it free.

•

He puts himself into his pictures, going away near
distance mountain slant. But all he sees,
including the "he's", is contained in a non-prefigured
boarded scope. You stand right before something
when you paint it. Hoping to put it away that
it won't go away. Feet on the planet.
Feet that feed a line through the top of anything.
And takes the sun in, and makes it his mind's light.
All pains to make the fluid solid, the solution
crystal.

To make the sex-engager as substantial as a
non-human, yes. The object of one's fancies, etc.
As plaque as right before a boarded furnace.
And what if she turns?

•

"I wanted to talk with somebody
I didn't know about flying saucers."

•

Do you know what one would be saying to
somebody like you? Would you know what
somebody saying it might know?
How sharp is it possible to be, being another?
The crystal waits like a reflective wand.

The reports came back from the detective band.
No use waiting around any longer, we should proceed
at once to the point of land. There would be
the light on a tall striped spindle. And there
would be our encased answer, but flying in a
still further wind.

Docks from the sea look weak.
Lights from the tide emerge and drown.
My hand was on the handle and my
shirt throat was wet. Don't blame
fuel for the dispersal of heat.

Flooring the car I entailed the engine to surface.

•

A plane of glass divided into equal waters.
Has it no existence if there is no language
however imprecise to fit?

The wind blows the rain in a great arm and hand
stain down the tree's trunk.
Why are there places where some thing is not happening?

A pointed building with tapering towers,
airplanes off to the sides.
The portions of strongest light tended to the opaque.
Therefore the so-called "light of reason" must be very dim.
"At this time, ladies and gentlemen, we'd like to play a tune . . . '
Written meaning condensed, no longer needing any light.
Exit the switch. Conclusion is vicious, like teeth
meeting strongly. Calculate the speed of reaching.
The light he kept lunging for from the dream could not
be pulled into existence. What do we suppose?
A technique for reading without any light at all, nothing
which could have been expected. A technique
for writing to the ultimate point of one's expectations.
Rounded unbalanced forms on a red plaster wall.
Eating one's fill and then explicating backwards from that point.
The hill was round, and the elephant also. So and
not so, check up on both. And then the universe
wherein "both" is synonymous with "same". How
easy it (would it?) would be to allow this all to
continue from any point in or on the crystal.
The men were currently sailors and had no knowledge of
wax.

How wonderful infinity! And how slanted, once
one's thoughts proceeded wholly from that angle.
Technique for driving a bell through the wall
without eliciting from it a single sound.

Once the being had hidden itself it proved impossible
to draw it forth on any subject beyond one of its
own independent involvement. No one knows
what it's like. Parallels now on, but not one
tangent. The tongue enters the mouth only to find
another already there. A discovery that
speech is never simply single. The radio in the car
received different wavelengths from the one in the house.
A closed system, beyond explanation or incarceration.
The teeth would have to be pulled though they had
produced no discomfort. A ways down the avenue
lay a log, and a little further along another.
The word "father" had been produced in the text,
significance pending.

The rabbit was large, larger, beyond the scope of the
present investigation. The handwriting grew steadily
smaller until he was dismissed from any further testing.
There was a red light in the laboratory window
which occulted according to otherwise withheld results.
I do not know if you know, but if you do keep silent.
A bridge amazingly large and strong considering the matches
of its construction. On the globe faces, more faces,
and beneath them still more faces. It really was
funny but almost none of them laughed.
The time machine proved to have the annoying habit of
continually involving itself politically. Salt.

Do you think you might pass it on to someone
that I have my doubts about the rest of this?
An uneven number of beats to the blues
will not necessarily cure your ills.
Nor will you surpass to know it.
Diminishing returns to the padded sack.

Something normative, something beholden
turns it back as soon as its number comes up.
We know, and we hum no endings.

•

And is this the same thing?
Nodded while doubting, and hauled it out into the yard.
Knowledge of squirrels, minimal, standing though hoisted,
spread out over a carpet of beads, close the door, squirrel.
He had stepped beyond his last. And then appeared at
the first. No known letters to impede his progress.
Oregano, stout. Loud voices though only on album.
The blood cells were repeated, as the trees the sky.
No erasures, no nothing pending. Entrance through
the hoarding, the penciling betrayal of stiffness.
Monkeys under the limit, the ground full of dirts.
Blank face, black avenue. The light rang
as he lifted his hand.

The crystal was white, yellow, silver, blank.
Transparence a matter of slowly mattering, coming
to focus under sun under thumb. You never
see beyond but through. Milky, blustery,
sheerly, coughs off down an oiled hallway.
Anything is possible, anything is undersung. Held to
be an oxide, held down under being lower. A
double one that repeats its index. Carted off
in chair, squirrel watching. Album bending,
match unlit. We see, and its mother,
the father of all hymns.

Marked cards, enablements to attach comment
or an elastic candle in firm disregard.
Cattle car mottled with starlings, fire truck
gilding out of harm's way a vote for fog.

And the amphibians we will all admit to being.
The crystal apparently on fire. The water
immediately on tap. The light. The light. The light
of its stone enclosure. She spoke, but
we listened.

There continues to be and has been lost, lost of
literary activity around town. But words or notes
or strokes or steps are not objects. But then
what is one? Something that backed into, or was
backed into by, the light and thus at first missed.
Now everything is missed and still standing around.
How can one speak from within the thought
of the thing, from the standing on the floor, from
the heart? Where is the source of the center?
How are the dreams connected, and where and
how weighty is their index? When I put it
like that all out of myself I perform a useless
repetition. Where bend the cards so they may be
listed in their shuffle? And how remember
exactly the leanings? Washfulness connected
to orange leggings.

I lost the mystery novel but caught the meaning
just as it was leaving. We have focused so much
on meanings we are left with maybes. And all
the structures have been left up, for the view if
not the hand. Perhaps the eye is beginning to leave
and the ear coming into its own. Perhaps neither or
both in the sense, what center of the mind between
them. The object, after all, is never just
red or cold. I took the mike out of the box
and played awhile with *its* alphabet. That I was
never out of my mind of the window. And how the
car comes.

Then dogs bark and the walls come true. The redness
was that of text but not of wall. Two things
occupying the same space of different sizes.
A thing occupying two shapes. Shape Master lifted his
hand from the sodden sign. Immediately thought
and put away. Immediately again. Immediately thrown
open to the glare and shut. The words in the cabled
message shut themselves off like beads on a plate.
The heads were still in bed in every frame of the Cadmium
News. Heads outlined in a reddish motion.
A not knowing anything by the saying. A largeness of
unspoken space for the taking, for the walking out, for
the wrecking after much intense building, for the openers,
for the nonce and the apple.

A wobble amongst three sentences. The church lived half
on its own land and half by the livers of its parishioners.
The walk by the way had been decided, by the waterfall
and its careful placement in cups, by the hand not needed
for a final allotment. The half-polluted cigars were
stacked by the river drained into. And another one,
a one of sod and limes and musical bracketing.
The one gone.

He docked by the crystal, pulled in all ropes and the book
could not be read. The crystal could not be white
for it was not seen. Sounds as if it was through.
But never finished like the unread book, the off-center
orange, the duck below.

And what is one's own death, locked as firmly as
a bubble in a crystal? A darker line I had
not seen before, product of facet angles, a
more condensed clarity, is these questions?
A question is a hand reaching. The crystal.

•

But I will not have the opportunity to do that.
I will not see myself later. On the average
no razor blades, no fans, no opportunities for
lifting the manhole and peering down within. But
everything, on the order of chaos, is possible. For
one, and the same me. The one out of order,
by the back door, the other. He needs no opportunities
for all is permitted, on the reverse side, the never
to be revealed to me. What I don't know
is the absolutely not to be known. I have no
sister. No brother either. There is now only me
and the same, the reverse, the intransigent
order. Out there loose in the all. And
no sense, I realize, in copying this out.
Under the city lies no space for me.

I keep spinning the crystal to see all sides
but I can never exactly see the side that is
turned away. In Japanese the haiku requires
17 syllables. In my language as many more as may prove
necessary. And it's a long enough night but never
that long. We pass from bit to bit, and even
exchange some of the bits between us. He lives
three avenues down, near the blue skylight above the
dirt factory. I pick up the copy of the book of
Thomas Mann I will never read. I admit same
to a certain one by letter. A volume of small
plays of a mechanical scent. Sea mice, gills
developed, under study at present. All the possibilities
in a grave and at once. Certifiable commencement.
Glands that produce laughter. Snails with seals.
Globes of clear dust attached to the palms.
Poems in a posthumous form. Follow the wake
before the vessel has left the dock. Trail
your hands before speech.

•

Wandering the earth, up and down in it, and in
its pockets the wand of stone.
A stretch of reaching until it burst its chords,
spill sand gems and open vaults in vapor.
The name was written on the package but not on
the letters. I approached the castle and
kept approaching it until I had no hope of
leaving it or of arriving either.
The keystone was balanced on an arch of cloud.
The waters lapped at the closure of any hands
at all. Morning. Folded lights. Terraces
as the pastime of enclosing plant forms.
Statuary broad as population at the favored spot.
The crystal poised to take my hand in its . . .

Crystal with the life of a broken skull.
Crystal with terraces for fastening cloud cracks.
Crystal contain the silver of its own crack of light.
Crystal raw and firm locked in air and my own plotted gaze.
Crystal with no answers to my questions, the questions,
        questions, salts.
Crystal with which to pick a rib.
Crystal no novel will ever enter.
Crystal with not so much as a name either.
I have removed the gathered name, it did not adhere.
The names were all shelved with their own shells.
The names were olden, of dated character, less than radiant.
The names kept track of each other.
Birds of a feather, capillary phrase, irradiant banter.
The corpse flowed long on a bed of splendour.
Color dry twig without the English u.
Names are preparatory, their legends strewn.
I picked up the name in an absent moment, gesture,
        cabinet door with a sprung hinge.
I raised the crystal, entered it in hand, locked the words
        from any thoughts to come.

I scratched and raved and slept.
I counted the take and found the crystal standing on the table o
        loss.
I was engrossed and it was left.
The lights to dismember, December and forget.

•

This book called the unread text might not be the one
the crystal reveals. The text of crystal might
reveal everything but itself. Readable as any plot
that shows a hole, a hole as central to itself.
The things not framed allow the mind. The crystal
continues to flag thought, and thought's belief in any of the
wisdoms. This book will not allow me to write
beyond itself. And less than a foot away
from these moving lines lies the crystal.
To catch the changes of its lights I must move
myself. Speed is essential matter.
The writer increases to any stop.
The crystal is not here.
I would be no longer writer of these words.

•

The crystal is possible as longer fingers are possible.
I reach out to grasp the fitting water.
There is no felt place for the phantom silver.
Through the top of the world the eyes unfocus
to differently shunted depths. Coffee
in the morning, smoke, coffee in evening, smoke
through the mind. Plain table wood and
elbow through concentric hides. The hole
in the noun. The hospitality of twin tears.
Slivered years to be held in one hand. The paw
that opens back the walls of the store.

He served the coffee in even rows. Pickles on
the sink, egg shells on the broken sill. People
will go to some lengths not to breathe immersed.
Change your shoes. Black shiny with white laces.
Change your tie. Peppermint candy stripe.
The leavings on the lawn were ignored by the dog.
The cat. The white-on-white skunk. And all of
July he dreamt of December. And all of January
she dreamt of that December. I wanted to see
you put the deposits back in their sample cases.
I wanted to see you inured to the law.
The law of sun and dark. The law of sessions.
The kaopectate bottle. The pink substance
smeared on a plane. They were leaving for the
southern corrections to their lives. It had been
furthermore previously ignored. Thoughts homing on
protrusions from buildings. The sky an after burner.
The secrets that were exposed at the party
nobody heard. Leaving the loaf out for the cat.

Clarity is madness. Is isolate damage.
To cleave off a facet for will dims the whole.
To take but a part is to spin the song to a single pitch.
To hear the wind as a howl. To see light as a fire.
The expert is the crazed mosaic, the blood-veined stone.
I must strike the crystal without touching it.
I must spread in the same light.
Nothing taken but what is
still now.

•

The crystal is the missing finger. How can anyone
see that far, as far as to forget what sorts
of meaning this might have had? All of them
seemed to be there and it was only finally

that he discovered what gap had been filled.
Finally? Merely another node of occurrence, concurrence.
One's own cycles, not the world's. As if it never had been
flesh, it still did matter. Conscience, earliness,
the fall of tubes in a venting wind. And all
afternoon, Parsifal, Parsifal. Minor and mindless
but sweeping provided the clue. The opening within which.
There are no streets here in the wood. The hundreds
of oldness that furnish the height.

Buried in a stream, or belonged from the beginning?
The house on Oxen Street with the boards stained
scarlet. Partially but not remarkably. It is
there, it is not unstrung by air. We must place
some survivable system in the earth. We must
come home again and again, endlessly same day.
Same night of the ceaseless thinking about it.
He is condemned to return, he is condemned to return.
As if one point on his table could return his gaze.

I see, I think, I work. I work I see, I
think. I think I see, I work. This is
not knowledge but extent. A precision bungling
of all thought matters. The dots that were
taken as eyes now periods, and they never
come in pairs. Perspective lies, the
universe has no one comprehensible form.
And yet to so much further all the further on are told.
The world is bold and glance and hedges. There
are insects crawling at the bottom of the invisible
bowl, mirror at the bottom of the brothel pool.
Our tongues are in our mouths and our hearts
are further off. Always. Store-bought articles
the substance of our books. The word our.
And the time of no pronoun. I think
I see it as all else works.

The definition of now is the false later
that all this will never take place in.
The crystal comes forth but once.
He is known, is he not?, for certain acts.
What else for certain acts? Perfect paints,
live words, nearby woods. Whatever light
holds even in an imperfect hand.

•

Face. Face. Make face. Believe face.
Make face believe face. Turn from it at risk.
Demise of life without a face. Prevent your face
from surprising you. Turn to it in times of . . .
Turn it in time, in time to avoid the seeing.
Revise face in memory, avoid the mirroring.
Keep face image from the inside feel.
Directions here for watching out, and listening for?
Drop face sense of life and plant as if feet
the forward plot of as yet incomplete disclosed intent.
Fight it out with face on a block before one
strange from the wall. Familiar. Own face is
one's familiar, as if an oiled path through
the air of the oaken cabin.
Cat at my feet, can it read my face?
They don't have those muscles.

Face. Receive on the sensitized parts the judgement
of acts. Arrange the frontal space as printout
of lies. Accept the cogs of another's expression
in one's own. Engage in conflicting act. Face
up (to), face down (another). A ceiling
is to receive, a floor an aggression.
Or brass tacks a simplification? or the music

is always in the air? These assertions in
words are neither here nor there, and face
nowhere.

●

A scarlet mantle, is it not? No, it is an
orange band. A scarf that is the weather's edge,
a rig of partial light. A flat of light and width,
a dimming strap that does not exist for those
in those mountains above which I view it. But
I am not over anything. I am back behind
over here. Impression of prepositions
additional to the certain enough effect. I could
write anything, couldn't I? I could hate
the light of a world for not dovetailing to my
taste. (How did those birds get in here?) I
could . . . I won't. The pronoun diminishes
in descriptional usage. The holes in the sky
are only the ones I make with the ones in my head.

●

"So nothing will ever be written down again. Perhaps
the act of writing is necessary only when nothing happens."

●

Battered by the crystal, lengthened by the crystal.
Traded off into a bulk version of my speech,
red lantern swaying from the rear protruding boards.
I no longer perfectly understand my own speech.
What I hear in my head does not any longer
synchronize. Blotting paper does not take a very
stark image. As if hearing the wind but once
in one's life, a single poem written. Correspondence

is not the general strew of things. Correspondence
is not in the usual direction. Dip the head,
breathe and blow through the slot provided and see.
And leer, and loom, and forget the shards of teak
once a widespread decoration. The edges of the sea
are bound up somewhere in this chunk of ice.
This landing stage blocked off by three dots at
each end. The tail of the crystal has been
wagged and a foolishness of aim become general.

•

And the clanking tree branches.

I approach catatonia looking into the horizon.
The rear protruding sticks are truncated not terminated.
As the crystal says, speech without blindness is worth little.
The crystal, it is dismembering me. Or is this all
something I am merely remembering? A question
that is not a question but seems to have all the
trappings of the question.

She stood up placing her fingers together over her head
and the breasts were pulled slightly in the direction
of the light. The shadows beneath the visible flesh
moving arcs. Body drawn through filters, the eyes
that produce nakedness. Shriek of an ordinary
car on the lower road. I am writing these things
to see if they can be seen, if not touched.
We were discussing the mineral residue of lust.

A gunshot in the backing cover, hands over the eyes.
Collapsing forms at the typewritten page, a list.
A sound, a solid focus, only one nipple at a time.
I tick off my limitations and rise, looking in the
eyes or only suitable facsimile. She smiles.

There are several hovers in that smile, the
expression of a form beginning to turn to my desire.
Light hands at night, dark array at morning.
I have the reputation of one who remains latest.
It was necessary to catch up with myself after
she had gone.

I began to rise but I could not leave.
Beginning to see, one leaves the world. Taking it
up again and again until the sheets are dark.
An inlet of the sea sharded with sails. The sun
coming up over a blinking multitude, specialty humans
provided for this purpose alone. I am the one who
stays up to see that they do not leave.
Cardboard hinterlands of the drained liquid trace.
Grey distances of chimney and low neighborhood.
Wet snap.

●

The crystals open like a rattle shaken
glisten in the stairway tapped
arrange for drum of size remove a wall
be witnesses inner of collapse barn stand
car and awl bitten in mast mist of a size tip
a tapestry drop stained of remembrance Spanishes
cap off the top of the Steinway driven in
sod stretchers and camels broughten
you see I hold it, crystal at the apex pitch
ram spark slaps of the touchen melodic
opening is belfry from the tick of the sword
and so advantage in capes and strand

The mist ship is the bucket space
the liars block at lipped paints
brass's pants furly sundialed

an ant in a capsule left town a b-b
an Anacin heft on Sen-Sen sufferance
and the Spanishes repeat their names in blond stone

•

And openings for the work to go in, and away and on
and the moments when it is not to write letters
(and you could hear disco tubs leaking from the gate beneath)
the flowers are on his cap as he points the notes
only spaces, like open crystals . . .
Thought there is in lumps. Lamps that fly
beyond the clothes. I cannot circle an o.
I cannot see myself eat. I uncap the article
and I go to sleep. Writings are small
strange walldrawings. Tomorrow will open the
strew with its play.

I painted the cap on my chest. To be shorn of
the crystal. The uncle that vanished in
aquarium ballroom. Marks that could not be seen
in the faint failed to turn him up. Perhaps
he did not go, he merely blended. (Accent on
the mere) Collisions in the mind are plain
on paper. I would have had to point and
move those walls.

To allow them to take over that space. The crystal
minds.

Put the crystal back in its cover, but there is no
cover or that is everything. The world smiles
away from the point, of dark. Of lock.

The blues are made of oxygen.
The crystal made of that, and something other.
And there is no labor of task in the clear paste.
And then it is heavier when still.
Fitting that the hand, does not fit. It lifts.
Tomorrow as blue as today. Breathing as well
as straight as the edge. The apparent tack
tomorrow and today take. Luck is caught up
in its whispers gelidly. Brokenly, talk.
Settled that it poise, shock and wait.

As luck would have it the sun was charring
the fiberglass tufts in the yard even from such a great distance.
A granite shithouse exploded in a cloud of bee odor.
The very earth was tacked to my wall, a ball of
limpid snails. Glass, blown firm, and then the
waterfall in the photograph it reminds me of.
Prose does not care about sharps and flats. It
continues to accumulate in the straightest of language
keys. I put back on my cap, it says. I lost
my things in the race for the car, it says. I am
not interested in the language of my past (my trail),
it says. It says these things and then loses
my interest. Two blanks curling in the same sun.

Why? No why. *Which.*

Perhaps I should keep the crystal concealed in my
clothes. But the strongest notion seems to be to
keep it at that exact point on the table. Why
have I left it there ever since I got it?
Motion for a crystal is not a matter of moving in space.
It directs all vectors it needs from a point.

Should I record things, or should I only wait
and listen. Should I open my reach, or should
I pretend meanings. Should I read any further,
or should I write only. The book awaits the
ringing of which pitch of bell?

Writing is a stillness with agitation digits.
Rock hums that only the eye can stroke.
The typing will make all this faster but the structure
will be similar. Counting all one's hairs and then
taking the pitch of the breeze that rustles them.
This useless activity is at the core of the work.
The crystal would seem useless to most current measures.
If I could write like the bulb with no noticeable
interruptions of current . . .

The balloon weighs as much as the crystal when
spoken up with all necessary breath.

•

The crystal falling over on the wooden top
sounded like two things falling over together.
Why should one lie in wait for someone?
The disc of ice from the barrel top placed against
the deck railing board vertical. Watch the sun
deform. What about me
wants change?

•

So going around surviving nothing so thinking of you,
perfectly slantwise crystal of the middle of my life,
my distance surely kept, enfolded in a slightly
downcast vision. And the world that is not
you, but dangling on, I live by the light
of your density, sharply.

The trumpet says out, so we get up.
I do it, my nights my days, my heart thrumming
in shortening prison, a prism, master of rays
and lefthanded as I am not. Yet.

The world is a baffle that shows through to
you, everywhere. Almost, and pieces of banana
left in nearly empty refrigerator. But for them,
for me the world dials sink, in daily drink
and some respite. Solace is not general. A joke
is not less than what it names. And the crystal
at the rim sits on my table, perfect to the letter,
one never sent, or kept either.

Crystal not survivable, but will remain me.
It lives in the sun-tipped palace of my regard,
until. One could place no period after it.
That I will change it, my challenge. Its challenge,
purefoot power of no regard. In back of the house
the washing lines up with the sun disc, one cold day
a life.

•

But does the light grow yellower in the crystal as I stare
harder, or has it been there as initial stain?
And now that I write this the flavor of its shards
glows again ice-white.
Do you want to know something?
How?

•

The crystal is the monad
and its volume a chamber
that merely lights on life.

It seems sometimes to become thin of sight
so that I almost do not see it
but still I grasp it all the harder
with something else.

Lights in the farmhouse go out regardless
whatever handle on the weather.
The regardless whatever is its essence.

•

Ice-white light just an inch above water
lifts the valley town and prints it in its own distance
as if I would never have to look at it again.
What is writing to this crystal that *stops*?

I order myself to present myself to it.
How arrange my hands, the print of my face,
the interlogging of my legs, the shaft of trunk
to what sunrise?
If I touch it anyhow it will take in my skin
to the blaze of its own imperfections.
It is perfect of imperfection.
The most perfect field a surfeit
of randomly bounding objects.
(as Keaton dodges them facing upstream)
My off-white pen scratches here
that I may enter in to that array,
morning opened into a corner of the underground.
The worst thing being a too few of the too many.

And the penetration of more than light.
Wounds of the body as ecstasy inroads.
My earliest masturbation over arrows drawn into
the bodies of cowboys in comicbooks.

A St. Sebastian vision of body penetrated by
long clear crystals. Great wand-cock of quartz
enters the mind . . .

•

I know you want nothing of me (there is no "want"
axial to you) and yet for some strange spacial reason
I need to ask you what you want me to do.
No doubt?, it's an ignorance of direction that
makes me phrase this as a questioning of you.
No reason to personalize a mineral but somehow
the words just come out in this way, as if I
could arrow them directly into you.

As it is late and you are still light.

There must be knowledge locked in you that I
could ask of no person. But perhaps all such
knowledge is death. I must want to
have it both ways: peer into you and keep
my humours circulating. I see my hand
passing through the barrier of clear substance
while still speaking with this pen.
Duality linkages, how well can they keep me?

•

Circuits of the Crystal

When I can see through into the outside finally . . .

Snow light on the undersides of the porch beams again
I stick inside these struts to think of
losing rhyme, losing cadence, the reverse, the imagined gnarl
the underpinned

the salt at the core of the snap
the bolt
the hold

             (tick, hum . . .)

the gloss cast that shines the gnostic weight

             ●

    "this perfect cube of empty night"

             ●

Far from honor to be seen here, languish desk ash.
Walked out into the night and saw things.
What? Heads. Embodied eyes. Anyway
eyeholes. Whistling solvent shaftways.
Insurgent lash hafts. And there was no laughter.
    (This is a mere gurgle on the page.)

             ●

The man polishes his things to have them imitate the
crystal's disposition. The form of the essay
with only certain facets that carry the light
to thought aggregates. The outside of all things
is cold. And light does not always depend
on heat, nor does motion.

The spun threads of certain ideas lock light
in the crystal. The crystal is turned, or one
moves around its outside to reveal them.
And yet so far I have seen nothing there.

             ●

The crystal is gone
into angles of an apparence I hadn't thought.
So does my hand also disappear. But I haven't
the ice to match it. Tomorrow it will
snow-rain. Today it cold-dried. I live until
I scream. What has been identified as
"the Devil" is merely matter. Matter
is collision, collusion, my confusion. There
must be a further state of things. Art is
merely the drapery, the task to scribe it thinner.
Perhaps this can not be seen or heard. Perhaps it
can be written? I want to pluck all
the hairs from my face, line them up and study them.
Not line them up or even look at them, much,
but know they are there and write. Write
about anything. The order does not matter
but the identity does. The crystal has its
expressions but they relate to no face. Expressions
of a ground source for further turnings of process.
The process. The sewing of the button to the pudding.
The shock that there was simply someone in the room
with him that had not come in and would not go.

It's foolish to think you can see into stone.
What you see is only what you put there.
Outside of the eye. The removed cooled gel. While the
window is blank. When all thought is mute black and you
feel the words. Catch those angles. Just enough to clear
the throat and then sleep.

●

The version of the story to the cave in the dream
said you will travel in a room to the rooms
within.

Vast glows of sponge-shred breccia loom
in the everlinked upper-unders.
We get in there to view them as are told
by the man on tap from his house at
the dry shunt of the upper-inner.
The dream clasps with botherages.
Clamp down of a single night
and there be no other versions.

·

The crystal is but one nexus in the drain
of speeded possibles. When there are fossils
on the bottom of every shoe. No place to store
the artifact, no sun to dial the seasonal reason.
Outside the rain there are other shards.
Minimal barns for cow flake and pig lozenge
and the whip in your face is a tongue of leaden.
I cower back I release my wall.
I encase my care, sink my cave to bloody
disparage. Stop this wick-strewn thinking.
Rear back from the past before each night.

But there are curious appendages to every thing.
They want out and into what. The readable
signboards were covered with burlap, and then lit
intensely with clip-on arc lamps. Clearly sense
to be made of the senseless, to the senseless
thinking themselves clear, in just such a crossbred
manner. Switch on the lights. Which lights
and where? All of them and the only chance.
Not much chance out of the total. All the holes
in all our nouns . . .

Senseless thing, crystal, say you of yourself?
And all the other things I say of you. Unto you,
and for you. Whichway and back. The metal
of the trains while moving painted to appear clear.
Don't bother tapping. You can see them moving around
inside.

If I could see myself, moving around in your
insides . . . and see what I'd see in there.
But it's not fair. You have hooked things up
that I could never see on a moment.
Now all I can see is you. Whatever you contain.
Whatever you do to time, not to mention
perform on space. There are to be no more
difficulties with space, I catch you whisper.
Or do your cleavages emit a gas that tacks a
bug to somebody else's ceiling?
The rates of incision are too fine to permit
the grasp of the gaping wound.
But what do I hear when substance freezes clear
like a die shot full of glycerine and the natural
polar powers of void seized on the eye?
There's a geometry to some sound almost word in the mind.

There are glittering sizes. There are sparks
that are cracks in edgy clarity. There's a
rhythm to parallels that notch off at
the ends, hazing with knowledge by the boards
you live on.

Change it all around. Place it on the notebook back
and make a crystal of black. Won't work, looks
like gum arabic in solution along one slant,
and along the bottom the striated shine of
a straight razor edge. Mask-making
for things won't be easy. By its lights, seemingly

ever on the change, it makes its way, holds
the needle glint of a rung bell up to my
wayward hand. Find another solution.
Breathe in a differently angled smoke, hear
the whistling of a snack truck bend uphill, and
watch the clock's locked hands. It's time,
as if it's never.

Looking back and then running forward, my hand
deteriorates. Or is it this stick of a pen?
I have breathed enough to be sure in my wonder
at most of it all. But this thing on the desk
has me stumped. No matter the thrust,
however much I spin it. And irritate
my eyes with its ballast. And rake my
brain with its tine, as if hair were all the
matter of thought one could pin up.
Rouge is not the color of bricks. Neither is
the crystal clear.

•

If you look into the prism you see the work
and window reversed. In camera the speech
revised. The man returns to himself backwards
the scene of all, the all of what happening,
the whole of that and the temper shattered into
apparencies whittled in revolved resolve.
What if nothing were motion in the flattened
version? The crystal quoth: Speak no more.
Say no further into what has been seen.
Words now needed to move the crystal.

The crystal as the passing-through figment of space.
As if the digit did not point but received,
not reserve, and sent on. But how much

revised? Reversed?
Again, again the coals lock over the sifting fire.
That light in the mind be a firmer light?
A grasper? After? After what fidgeting lunk
on the prowl?

Collide the eyes with present tenses
and be off to see, prime to veer
and chosen as the heaven one admits to standing up.
The fragmentary is the whole for now.

●

Adults who wouldn't believe the crystal hadn't been
cut and polished. Joshing sessions.
Then admissions beneath the elbow. The cellar.
You wouldn't have had to tell me what I
hadn't thought to say. I could have gone out
to the day, the open hall, the thoughts of speech
all dissolved out there into it all as clouds.
Day. We collapse and speak. Jerk.
Enabling lessons, and the certain tower the remnant
of a trunk. That I hurled to admit
the crystal. The point of minute returns.
The grenade enclasped in the forehead.
The entrance of a sheet to all drills.

Admits to hearing, admits to wearing . . .
All those facets buried in the moon
and what some other woman than your mother just
barely has on. Stop saying, stop doing.
Rest.

Writing in a vast book, the exigencies of
the stopped snail. Brighter and brighter and then
reft from hearing. The night is as dark as

the inner stains. The brought-off bolt in the wall
turns into my stare. Nothing as pitiful as these
drifted dots and lines. Furls and shares.
The elephant on packing hand.

Pre-numbered, but no other language.
The silver gleams clear. The house has come loose
from its standing objects. But I foresee
no complaint, other than the wrist watch
on the drumming hand. No obligato
is obligatory. Under clerestory.

●

Two blocks, as far as you
can see through, can come to
the thought lights out
as fast as cracks
and the belongings radiational

Sliced through as a sigh visit
to the site, blank, of the last look
and as usual and seasonal, it was in twain
the volumes that neat up to holes in the hill
the head

The night is fact blank, not so
rational, and not so visible but clogged enough
you go right out through the wheat rate doorway
and the hand rejects the foolscap figures
after tracing them then through the drum

But at the level of height line curve of hill
what is that single?

●

"to write is to name silence"

•

And to name age and to name rights and to name
all the slots and implacables that prevent you from
writing and keep you at it.

To write is to say this. And to write is to
write out into the all about you. Where your
self is never seen but seizes you.

•

The crystal is the single before you of the more
than many. There is the one, the two between,
and the many which is also the more. As infinity
is the beneficent limit. Then the project is to
place the single, the crystal, precisely *at* that limit
and see where and what that horizon may lift.
Moving on from the infinite means exactly that,
and thus takes infinite means?
That I have infinite means presumes all the remnant
action. That I have limitless ability perishes me,
perishes the thought. The crystal is the line where
preclusion includes, as inclusion precludes.
All crystals turn on the tiny axes of inclusion.
They are its points of light. And the thoughts
sparked by them inform this writing.
And all the time I am using my hands
in the musical dimensions and as barriers to
the writing. If only I could spell myself
beyond ability.

There are thirteen letters to my name.

•

Be ready to build the boards to your rafter ear.
Light off into silence later. Submerge in tendency
obliged. Wheat off the light into a brow of
crystal, which is not ideal just a drowned berry.
The rates across are not the same as a slumping off.
I admonish, myself. I say that crystal
admonishes me. I tell it that. I want
to hear not as if, but *that*. All sayings
start off grounded, you have to lift them, learn
dispersal to round on substance. What comes out?
What tells me anything? The mind begins to
grow in edge.

Pituitary investigative rank silence.
The realm entitled "Name Silence."
The error of the pen hand makes it
"Bile Once." The opening of the eye in a
lemon covering, a barn of rustled threads.
You are not so sure as silence, not so many.
Not so much as the hand does you will learn.
Not so easy brought to thought as the hand
questioned toward the brow. To make up a link
of the loops in mind. Bury the trowel, that
borrower! Sun of world will not so easy cut
these mind parcels, braided in lunge, and so
capped any hurry would not hurricane it.
How and when do you spell it?

All thought in silence whispers, like phosphor
drawings on room.
The stillness of the crystal says Time, time is your
medium. And time is also the fallenness
of all your virtue. Your wand wending on.

There are thirteen facets to this crystal.

●

Still the sentence is hard won.
One has to fight through to the sentence
through the crowding and disparate ones.
Only spiked and jostled on the way does one achieve it.
Some of the words are sharpened and must be coaxed
and laid back into their velvets. Some should
not have appeared at all and appear to know it.
Some come too easy into use and must be questioned
and most discarded. The numberless ways weary
the mind's hand. It is always late and dark
and one seems always about to settle.
Give me some unfastened knowledge.

The winds increase and some of the ice
will thin but not slip. And if the winds
bring sleet then the ice will increase.
And tomorrow everyone will slip and curse,
the orders of the winds.
Will an ice night make of the window
a paler black? All that multitude of
crystal slanting down the winds, and this one
here before me stationed I barely glimpse.

Reading all sorts of novels in the midst of
each other and at once. Japanese novels.
Oregonian novels. And not forgetting where all the steps
and inroads go. This may be one of those tasks,
they told us, for when you're older. When
it doesn't seem to matter so much if you forget
things and so of course you find you don't.
When it should matter all the more. When you
wouldn't want to find whole teeming cliffs of
forgotten matters looming over you, memory loss
on the increase. No, I want to see the
one thing in front of me, known.

I want to hear the one thing speak that
cannot speak.
I want to know the things that can't be known.

I want to speak only here in this closed book.
To hear those sorts of things said, that can
only be spoken in this sort of closed silence.
When the rest of the world is not awake to any
of this, and I also would rather be sleeping.
The wind making its marks on the other side of day.
And the crystal only keeping its lights, to itself.
And to me.

This is already endless but can never stop.

The snow is already almost completely gone.
It leaves the dirt again.
But it stills nothing in its leaving. The winds blow.
The ground here dials itself toward the future.
It radiates up toward my hand and seems to bring
out words. But none of those words ever speaks of itself.
I do that. I am able to speak of my materials
but all that is immaterial. And I think of
the mercury in the tube, unable to decide which
way it will go. Next will come more winter.
And then spring, and then more spring. Summer
will be but an aftertaste. The high seasons
are but residues of the transitional ones.
Some of the writing will appear still, but it has
only been dropped by the ceaseless motion.
Lock hands then, even if only your own.

•

His head was raining. His eyes were in the
crystal. Everything was going by the darkness.
The crystal could have been a blade in all of its
aspects. What is to be done with
the clear ice of an absent air?
Not so absent, filled with a swarm of thoughts.
You should not fiddle with things as they are.
No matter that at once they may all arc in the air.
We *are,* said everything. And we have not really
noticed, said the others. Those whose breasts
primped to be noticed, and those who were not
noticing them. This is not wholly a dream.
But then what is not? Later than night and
later than the morning, the rest of the day will go.
My thoughts will pass over whatever motions
my hands will take more times than might
be thought possible. This table is a world,
considering the edge.

The nail head is gleaming in the light wood like a drop
and the full moon is straight out. Light cloud
mists it a bit as much as my lack of glasses.
Everything is refined. Meanwhile the crystal sits
on its hands. Some do rest on whatever past deeds.
It's refreshing to wonder if the winter succeeds more
than past winters. It's a wonder that the window
received everything, no matter the vector, uncritical.
The cat remaining outside and the crystal in.
My eyes are in my head, my edges. My thoughts
do not land. The whole world a floating wish
at two in the morning. And these sentences,
who cares where they break?

●

Will the crystal drain out poisons from the body?
That it is at hand. That nothing may strain our
relations. The grey agate of the afternoon sky
against the blackening tree trunks. There are warm
places of light in the tightening overcast. I have
sleep sometimes and dream, and othertimes speech.
I read the books and I melt the ice. I
ingest liquids and I talk to the visiting persons.
I tell myself that I have my reasons but often
they seem hidden even from myself. I talk
to the landscape and I enter that here.
There is very little that I can keep in a box.
When I was young I wanted to learn to tie knots
and I gathered nautical volumes of same. I like
to watch wires against the sky. Can you believe
what you had once heard about yourself?
Can your thinking be all there is to ask?

Knowledge flows between the known and the unknown.
There are flowers whose names . . .
And a large chunk of mineral of a green
and heavy and whose light . . .
Silence in the presence of the occulting lights.
The crystal behaves as if . . .
And it was said, all of it, that . . .
One sentence does not know what of the next.
Three people could come into the room, or two,
or none. Music could turn cold in the boiler
room. A large chalk of rose hovering in the
ashen place. Somehow the tip of this pen is
never cold. Sometimes I hum melodies I can
put no words to. Often the grammar escapes me.
Last year the wall seemed closer and its stone . . .

The crystal of the slanted terminus and the words
of a certain slant. Everything you know has been
urged back into its place. I am on vacation
here in my own house, I never write anymore on
loose sheets but in this notebook. I'll have
a time when I read it all through later.
I'll have to expunge, I'll have to accent.
But should I eliminate the sky and keep only the
trunks? And not stop to think about any words
while I use them. Enter the place of cold stones.
And the fused ashes, and the music of the rose.

Wrote which I was sure would do no good.
No apples in the farm but in the flame for all
we could do to stem them. Exact but unequal notches
in the fluted columns, an old recording anyway, not
precisely entirely forgotten. You move up on your cigarette
each time you hollow it. The day after the day
the computers fouled. They lay by the lake awake
and did not avoid the reams of names or forms.
The forgetting of everything is on my list today. That
and the sun, the moon's tilt, and the everlasting face
formed to the left. We have forgotten our schooling
and enter the rules. All day every day far away
and near. And these thoughts to be copied out
in the lighted shadow of the crystal.

Rain pours from the glare on one facet of the
crystal which serves as a fissure. All the
connections are not made within the sentence.
Everything I have said comes back to me as smoke.
All the diminishing pages. The lines between eyes,
between ears, between summer and winter. Between
the crystal's body and the window's thin height.
In the dream I drew out a stone and sharply tapped
the skull just above the right eye of Neil Young,

who was a woman, which was a black cat.
The animal went still in a flash, as if never
to move again. I was the only one in the
attending crowd who had known what to do
and I had stepped forth smartly and done it.
But often rapid knowledge leads one wrong. And
everything had gone out of the eyes but a reflection
of light. Such knowledge is too frequent.
A single nail in the firmament, a listening post.

•

"A dead man's face can tell us better than
anything else in this world how far removed we
are from the true existence of physical substance,
how impossible it is for us to lay hands on the way
in which this substance exists."

•

The crystal's facets have parted time
and allowed perfect stillness to exist.

Or perhaps stillness is perfect time
condensed and held in such substance.

I look into its light, a light which is
neither absorbed not reflected.
It is poised.

•

Down the hallways into the carbine of the sun . . .

A great number of Japanese novels
full of space and tiny points.
Everything can happen in them and nothing overlaps.
People notice things and others write them down.
The sunlight the moonlight and the earthlight
The insect

•

Could the crystal turn to the precise point that
I could not see it? As in the story where
the man is so thin that when he turns sideways
he disappears? Useless to search for that
notch on the perimeter. Somehow it bothers me
not at all that I do not even want to find it.
But does it please me that such a task is useless?
Where did I go?

Is this the only way I can now speak, arms
on a board to a dumb stone? The silence
of written words is perhaps correct for this
connection. An off-note to think of oneself
shouting against wall of crystal. Better to breathe
on it, dampening and misting its striations. Best
to be writing (whatever?) here in this book
in its presence. The window glass is but a
gross imitation of the crystal, as speech is of poetry.
As a closed book is the strength of a hand
brought to a perfection. Poetry is the closed voice?

•

The crystal cannot speak. The good book cannot speak.
Only the hard white strip at the edge speaks loudly.
Fill your hand. Draw.

•

What's all this holler about speech, don't you think
they know? No, a careful enough even around
the edges consideration, they do not.

·

Well why not? It's a good book.
I live these days to read, and to thought.
To be barreled by on bridges by staffy avenues,
holding off the still sense of stuff. Travel.
Losses by the brimful, standing out in flats
hankered and not hugged. Monstrance on my lapel,
mountain there to peel. If I thought of you
you'd turn broke too, and eye me back across
whiskered blots.

There is acreage around dunes which is the reading
as a youth of Wolfe. He suns himself as I do
in need of letters. We reel each other the deeds
of a stuffed-up life. Later they'll be saved in attic
barrels and loaves of remembrance. Thoughting it out
till the till shakes and we're mad at our loss of
boated days in grey lot city. Exciteds in apparel,
conversant of the sticks in life by none but us.
A nail skipped off a bus. Three stones next on
the same side with green doors. Handles that are
brine seals on the scouted poem. I walked into
basements and saw balloons of exit fission, red in
the back and asleep on a lark. Father Phister
emitting his bulbs back behind the fog and fan factory
when evenings they laid out docked china and had
themselves a paid laugh. One knocked over the ocean
and sold his boat, walked away forever into thicket
New England of brought ice turned into new green house.
Another plans wicked bop pranks in the L.A. smear.
Swale. The Brothers Fandango, say goodbye to Connecticut.

Land me on my feet in Lumpskin Prairie, far from
the nodule mobile on Tom's Peak Bulge. Radio.
The flutters won't wait for a cage.

I'd already known of the crystal then.

Cap me back in the pen then, it's almost the gate of a
new year. Hello. Trip over the marsh and map your
deltas, take savagery to be a sharp leather pocket,
tie your hands up to the amazement line. There'll be
stuff, lasting to tumble, oh yeah. Write everybody
one more time and slip away forever. Gratitude is the
last line.

●

"The Already Stars"

●

But could it all finally be as baffled as a floor?
I want to see what I'd finally say
at the base of the crystal. Knees to the convex.
Might I wrack my mind with evasions of smoke?
Peer into torment tomorrows? Ashcan out the window
of alley ox-cats? Who'll ring my tin-head?
Startle over the stars from basements? Is all my
crystal mind a congeries questive?

Settle down in cigarette bath and bang the list and listen.
There'll be monks excoriating. Aisley heaven, bank on it.
Clash of flate rats and stolen. Vivacious brink bouts
on chrysanthemum and votive. Howl down vodkas
and limp to rusted weddings. Tilt creosote as a seer.
Refine this pen. What the ceiling needs is a
tough perfume. I haven't thought about the thing

so I'll bow to say it. And learn to spell
at age pretty well. Needling fluted dressings
of the aid bat.

●

The crystal speaks: I don't know you said.
                    I know you thrown.

●

The mere flick that changed everything.
It's in there, it doesn't wait.
And don't concern about the roofing bulb slice.
Bearing it has, but not on this. It changed
the wait. We no longer thought. Who's this we?
This self that is. Could you imagine not being
the number one? What if the while it
poured rain?

●

Missing things, here and there. The slice. The block.
The check. Change cymbals, change pencils.
Start out at the wall and lurk up. Think only of
the glad aisle of openings maybe. Dark
decimal dowel holes, and haunting owls of the oilboard
wall. The turnbuckle stop. And then missing
every thing but you, silica chosen.

●

It's only his big blue pickup with the one oily hole
and I thought I'd shot it but it only ranked up
buzzing in distance and hullabaloo hums
the stairs timed themselves

Just got caught up in all gorgeous greens toward the sky
miles sward toward night, and in the teeming loomings
of the bedded kid, bedded with nothing, bedded
in snow ash

It's bright, but that bright is dimming
and it nodules toward that all-out hole
that dimmer valence thought out by trees
coiled by the cold throat the knees make of thighs

Limitless blesser domes
and hulled peas
you all wanted to see me but
I mastered hulk beyond school
and its black

●

Negligent in its brightness, French poetry.
Notionless of its fill, the crystal.

Entrance to sack plugged by dictionary.
Route toward land only through waters.
I open my mouth, and stalk.

The crystal at the lips is a jet stripe of firm.
Has no hold. Crawls in the tube
of the tree cut down. Molds the more
nothing says. Proves poise as doubt
the curve of a hand.

I have limited myself
here to the crystal, to everything
among the missing.

●

The crystal is the Key to Time
stolen

The man whose head was on
shadeways

The brads at the bottom of the gloss breaded
with words

The gist
the memory owed

•

Are we going to
have some snow
now we may
but not now

There is too much ice in the crystal.

•

The memory mumps contend with flattened steers
It's all in the college lesson with the candle collar
In the utopia of the tentacles we gained starving
In the house without staves and shoes we shunned

I would go to live with gravid begonia
The last laugh I knew was in the cab of a fossil
The salt kept slipping from the stockings of my volumes
As I hurdled the crystal and held up an itch

You have not told about this
You staggered this apple pit with January ash
And smoked the axes
You strand

•

Better you held water
sphere to your reach
than drained it
to its central stone

•

These lateral lobs sent to mind by the French
explain nothing but a brain porous to the lyric
on a night without water without hinge without moon.
I lower my temperature, my lids, and my cigarette
and blow this long at the facets.

What do I own, as the French own the lungs?
I even loan my cigarettes out
as if exchange were a drying process.
There are lumps in the fingers after
writing but nothing in the chest.

Printed love is article-dense.

•

Malignant in its brightness
rotting forms silvered with mould
snail slime trail on my hand
brought out under the glass of the bulb
and looking into
it to see what pronged the daylight down

Damage of Image and resultant
the urge to grasp

The urge to pinch, and leak sense
to fold dense and eye oneself
to swelter in the following
loss of names

●

The stillness of knowledge, that it should only come to
an accumulation. Why does it not stir at least the
surface of the pool?
He wanted to know what would happen if he put the
crystal in his mouth. He wanted to know what
would happen if he left the crystal on a railroad
track. He thought he knew that. He wondered
if the crystal would still be warming in the sun after
all the humans had died. He imagined it standing
on a sandy plain like a fire in the fire.
There seemed beauty in this but no knowledge.
Nor any motion.
Will the motion contained in these words continue?
To insure that, he put them away.

●

Crystal Solace. The room with one central
unlit candle.

●

The still distance
   of sweltering toads at the turns
the crystal on to your natural facts

●

Writing without thinking
of the repercussions
the marks that list against you
everything

Lifted into story it is airy
and does not weigh

•

Awakened by a bang
or sudden rent of room
a collision of the thinking with
where the thought is not
or negative moon spot
or release of the chimney from
behind the pie tin, night
and left partial, face erased
prepositions for furniture

•

Nothing is appropriate. Only rice. And banging tin.
Once was thin but now have thickened. Oil paper.
Miserable ideas, thin but functioning, ocean with low wick.
Thinness of light, a skin on the crystal's facet, the one
that shines in shard waves like a window running
in rain. Living close to the rain sometimes opens one's
mouth while dreaming. I have never yet dreamed
of this crystal. But will this writing take me there?
I shake the light across the facet by turning my head.
Writing is all reflections. And said reflections' stilled
connections. Learning and this is like running among the drops.

•

High nerves from wanting things. Listening to the water
and running fingers over a book of desire. Thinking to let
the back flap. I have something to steady me, a
single. But the mind goes out to the ends of
all turning. A fluting of space, making halls into
wheels. The words must be set one next to another.
But not the crystal. It was born in density with many
of itself in a chattering space, cold vug all dipped
in points. Someone plucked it out and rounded its base.
Now it spins in my sight, and under my writing.
It contains time. It is the space between two nerves.

•

I accidentally catch myself in the glass
and it's someone else standing out there in the wall
or yard of books, a teenage kid in bric-a-brac
check shirt and beveled forehead, hair shock black
as night its part, seems to move just a touch
independent of my own moves, though I know every
second who he is . . . Do I not?

•

The shape of it with me everyday, never the same.
It draws it out, the poem.
And is shocked of light at my tap.
How much is too little enough or at all?
Somewhat, a febrile word. And how many
words to produce a sword.
The crystal in the glass would twist me no difference.

•

"the crystal does nothing"

•

But what do I do? I wake in the morning, late, usually
feeling like I've risen from nearly drowning, glance
at the thermometer if it's winter, if it isn't
ignore it, get to feet, strange phrase, as if
feet were a verb, at least they're transitive enough,
proceed to bathroom, splash water in eyes, that's
intelligent, to see *better?*, and writing this way makes me
feel like I'm delivering my retarded valedictorian
address, no matter, put on itchy bathrobe,
walk down dark hall to livingroom and kitchen, draw
a glass of orange juice, if I've remembered to
fill the jug with frozen the night before, and toast
two english muffin halves in the cheap electric oven
that requires the button pushed down twice, consume these
items while listening fuzzily to idiot talk-show radio,
checking for some weather through the big glass
western side of the livingroom, walk
back to bedroom, arrange cloth on body, and then,
and only now, am I ready to start scratching down
words on page after page of

What do you do? Know the word "compassion"?
Sounds like a sheet of white-hot pasteboard.
That won't do! Try again.
A feeling the words have for each other?
You're like one of those people has to
go back to the beginning, each and every one.

•

"The elephant of the Jardin des Plantes has been
slaughtered. It wept. It will be eaten."

•

Well, now we have no method and the crystal is as clear
as unmixed air.

●

Bring me something out of the wadded future
and get home with it okay safe, the book with the
anklets and jeweled finger guards and the anteroom
for pausing in, no furniture but rose quartz
on the boards, window higher than you could
see through to anything but sky patch, cold
and filled but with warm spots, soak,
muse, flume, go away just
as another day's been. You have.

●

It's nine below fear on the shortening decks
as hand reaching for cat tips the stormware.
Time to go out, even if you are.

●

Sure coils of gone smoke
brief current films
you'll have to go outdoors to look back on your life
I tell myself
I burn

●

How to fill up so it all floats
leaving commas on the sea
leaving you near enough alone to me
speaking without hearing but touched

by my own rush tongue inside
needled by verse and beaded by prose
neglecting my handwriting and satisfied

Makes me feel old and fresh

•

Hey, tundra bear! echo of cardamon seeds
the limpid vapors that rest on glass have destroyed
and I limp off thinking about berry papers and trunk

Wild overjoyed bull weevils and violet snaze
the glass ball in my head fogged with Sen-Sen and pinks
I let the photo-bulb off and myself in at the door
that night is always singular is shown

Franked that syllable with a blot of my hand
so it won't be missed or colored or read
the yellow vellum glove of the literary world
closed with a safety pin

•

Brubeck,
          Just how long were your mistakes?

•

The Aurora:
The coldest light, the daughter wondered if was hot
A northern horizon glow spread to zenith
     in blades of shifts, arcs erasing and crossing
          shadow with shadow
A lit wind

as if a light were moving behind the sky
    behind shattered objects casting their shadows on us
You're almost more aware of the shadows, the shapes
    where the light has just been
The motion you can't follow or predict
What forms this racing of interruptions?
    mockings of the solar wind
It pales then brightens and tinges just the edge of a spectrum
A fanning of stills
    that speaks to the frozen things
These ghosts of light, darts of shadow
A pretense the shade of some lamps
    that got caught out and baffled
and you're not there, and no one anymore
    the surface all polar, only the flicker left

•

Was the aurora like light viewed from the inside of the crystal?

•

Going somewhere and not thinking about it, just leaping
I wonder. I need, and turn the page, the thrust
edge of the law. Imitation of nothing ever
to be seen again forget it, and in parallel?
I want to know what whether to do is. And
I am speaking, thinking, thought to say something on the phone
The syllables are not here for me to hand them over.
They are in place and disturb, I am not, am hobbled
in a wonder, in cross-hatched but viable bode.
There is a place to be gone to, but not beyond, the
crystal. I am the one who removes r's as
he goes, as he thinks, as not to go anywhere,

as he forgets so leaps. The intentional garden
or guardian. A not knowing I could put before me
a foot. A late night. Leaden phone.

•

Do you want to read *all* of the signs?
And do the colors bother you? Are you like me
in the coming together of far newer and near old words?
I had thought that the auto would give you an alternative.
Spend is the word, I had thought of it. I have heard
of many others' decisions, careless they seem to wend,
pretension all over the lot. Fare of the kind now
and again. Going off a bit, aren't you here?
Always. Offerings.

•

The crystal key: to turn the page, the edge and throat.
To bear the result of having decided not and then just gone and.
The universe is done. Things appear and appear to, but
they have been here, have guided us all along. The
sill of the tongue, the sharp serrate of musical weeds.
And desires are mixtures, them and us. Long tones
that snap, and then you have what have you.
The crystal long been and hum as if an ice.
But it is not but that has been there here.
The lines of light of bubbles too small to see, or
to see by. My glasses are too large to read by.
With a possible verb. How and when or why,
nouns. A key to unknown, that frictionless
nothing. Goodbye is a song.

•

You fall forward and there is no floor, a wall.

Don't know, don't even see, hear.
Place and hear the weight of light in a handful.
But it is hardly a handful, almost a point.
Not a surfaceful, determination of color and position
on the land and bell-like wall.
Do you really see as I can hear you seeing?
Might all be a resistance to the flying from images?

●

A city where everything is patched, where eye wanders
glowing over remnant, and where the vents of parsimony chew.
Nothing ever brighter than blackness in motion.
Nothing more telling you than the storms of broken time.

●

Dream of a fossil sea animal in matrix,
round and flattened at the top, we peel the layers
away and find the interior sections still living,
or just rotting? Thin layers like a meaty baklava.

●

Not known of anything in the blur snow drifts
on land under woods out to the sneeze of
                              horizon lifting
Grasp of any form is overrated
a hover, not enclosure
nothing has the weight of safe in the head
and there is no minding what light draws

●

An orange belt that instincts the radio
band for enclosing whims and rates
pins the lowness to the inner
hand at the edge
flash
of solitaire
coughs in the air

●

The sun a pinhead a lighthead
a bulb too wiped to allow much
hurled and flying on its own ball
reminiscent ovum, strayed shot
lets see, a little lets hold

●

Not knowing what to do but seeing the terminal ice,
the glass in which more of itself is filtered shown.
Not much more than precise angle and no roof, a pitch
but to which key of what matter and not dependent
even on light. And I go on seeing all of the
things and nothing to do with. The hat of iron
in a folky stall, the coils of the precision blanket
where I drop my head. And in darkness of that
just the one name.

●

Inside the involvement of violet windows, stress
in hand and on pumps of think it over back all
again right, decimal plots on fictive board.
I'll line it up said-so on vegetable tablets, in
rink-tongue halls, at batches of spiderware calypso,
by last bulk of recede peck no longer of

trains emittive the line has slit them so flare.
You'll blunt out behind bulkward avenue
that I but see you and you inch. That other
you is me. And shut planetarium go on refining
for the empties.

●

He wanted to walk outside. So he left the door
and went. To the next issue, these are fraughtnesses.
The word looks astride and so, there are partial openings.
For the farm for the knuckle for the lift that parallels
the sun turned into meat at the pen. Otherwise
than angling at the crystal.

Otherwise than sound afternoon, exceptional of
false grasp at type of tongue, and if rhymes
with Monk the crystal pinks, the emergent brothers.
The sunderances. The long of life.

●

You must avoid thinking what is said so loudly over
only portions of it which you must see, use own
eye ears original mind. This is the lesson of
the crystal: I was there and I saw, my proof.

●

A life lived in primaries
a shout from the center of the light
no secondary lines

Call off your ridges, I profess the peaks.

●

It hangs there. It turns itself up to our eyes at
the edges. Whose eyes turn themselves up at the corners
would see it also. It is not even the moon
we had thought we would see. It is the glasses
of a young Stravinsky leaning back against a felt-covered
board. I don't know what happened, but suddenly.
The clearer quicker writing necessary is needling me.

Then the eye in the crystal moved.
I picked the crystal up and rubbed it both ways across my
brow then down onto the bridge of my nose.
Anyway it would shine like the blade of a knife
with forgotten use. Rows of centuries, the reflections
across its facets. If only I could recall uselessness.

•

The crystal tides in stranger gravels by a roadside.
Though I would it would lamp. Dayfiller.
Rottens wooden from bottoms of trap. If it all were
to cleave? Photo clogged sphere like sulphur emission.
And needless or never to be strived for you will be published.
The crystal a reporter. The memory a sky the former gravel
has pressed.

•

It doesn't make any sense to behave before your light.
But there is an increase at the very least.
My feet have changed their rhythm, or my ears take
more threat from the silence, or all my thoughts
relate more closely to one point, or the heat makes
the light of the room seem blander. These are all exercises in
a tonic possibility, one which may take me further
toward . . .

•

I can finally write the word "belief" here.
I believe that the crystal is where I left it,
the exact point at which I last saw it.
In that sense it can be said to *depend on* me.
My knowledge of it, however slight so far, has
become its life.

●

Outside it rains, what had been frozen.
On another field the smoke writes in itself.
And in the air the crystal's pronunciation is not known.
I have no freedom from my own.

●

A little separate loop in the grey unction
and if it eventually goes it will not wend.
Laced down by a high chemical stripe
it does, not breathing, not breaking the plane
though washed in by walls, impossible to stand to.

For this is not the place to be, from which the light,
in which undoubted matters.

A very large cape with eyes hidden in the transparence.
This was seen and then it was heard that one report
of the view was in error. Offshore the board
floated vertically unaffected in its elements.
We see through nothing. The paintings all with black borders
on the adjacence of the volume's pages.
Large sides hide pleasure. Leavings of which this sun
has no part. The one of the ring at the top.

●

The crystal very shallow today
no light much past midnight
no part in the shadow I make
half standing half shorting
the words (not there)

•

But saying how water looks is like a light piece of ice.
Talking as if you knew it, the crystal waiting.
How can it be so silly as if to think
I want it lurking, reacting in human tones.
It lies, it stands (for what?) not much better
(or lesser) than either (which?).
I am calling on my confusion now to handle me.
Focusing all my . . . on a single . . .
It's later and still the light has not gone out.
I'm very quiet and I'm not remembering.
I'm not waiting either, just listing slightly.
But the crystal is not a mast.
It's very. It's completely. And the chief holds out
a piece of cold.

•

The gem weighs bucks.

•

He just walked in and sat down. We didn't know who he was.
Just those dark eyes in a light complexion.
He spoke: "Hold on." His hands flattened on
the rough plank arms of the chair. We hadn't noticed

it before either. The background grew blonde.
Were there windows? Was it even daylight or were
there lamps lit somewhere?

•

And if the light is applied
spin the crystal at the base of the brain
the stem, or tongue
could this will be
absorption or erasure of
all latches?

In sun, in wind
which is all remains
of darkness, a feeler
that tells me little more than
that a little more hand
is mine

Movement is the hidden
apex of the stillness
the crystal tends

•

But is it all enough to tend upon?
Where are the seams in the evermassive holding?
Time appears to lie late as the solutions
silt themselves dry, flatten.
The car turns up the road, the light coils into a blank.
And I feel cold enough to be the last witness.

•

It's clear that this has nothing to do with.
Sides that curve of the flesh a tone, a carve block
in shed liquid and fire plain returned.
You do not finally see but wholly fuck.
And the crystal hives a cold that does not
remain you. It loosens everything but itself.
The hip sheds fill.
Emollient that keens the spreading off.
And in the sex kilns the smack turns through and smither.
The key does not keep the time.

●

Watch out, you'll cut yourself.
But he's told us *nothing!*
Inside the hold, once there, you'll see.
I haven't covered it, I'll never cover it.
The one time that that happens, people tend to forget.
Nothing on top of nothing, a certain civilization.
The rules, why, they come from somewhere else.
If I could see the light, but I've never thought about it.
The news came from further but never further enough.
And I was helpless, I knew.
Peoples' teeth . . .
In the wake of the understanding, sheer pitiful continuance.
A man inside there, don't you see him?, help him.
Commands to stand, and then commands to stand some more.
Looking down from the top, forever, into the future.
And side by side we talked, and walked, and thought to stop.
It's *not* free, it's connected.
The walls did not move, you only thought.
Permissions, to continue, on other ones' laws.
I opened my hand, and the thing was, it was missing.
I copied off the rules, of the thing that just stood there.
At sea, on the land, in the air, as all still holds.
And drenched, that it mattered, and didn't, and did.

So bruised, I spoke on.
The words that centered inside grew mist.
Might have been a blueness, at the edge, of that last crack.
An opening, finally, filled.
Small things, dental work, impending gleam.
And looking through it that way, my fingers were clean.
Diminished substances, roofing material, water in sluices.
The ring that was never figured, procrastinated.
The short and the long of it, humming.
My writing here, clear, askew.
It's too long, for the light, it'll never match.
Went to the island, came back, still on the desk, bubbles.
Bubbles in trim, encased, driftless thought.
I knew what you were talking about, but I never
        dreamed, the diamond window.
And the fog on the frost on the mould.
The night creatures in the lap rug.
The bell that rang deep in the substance, the worry.
And my hurry, haste, quickness to divulge and care
        to hide, whatever case it came in, apparent.
Unclear, below decks, light before your eyes,
        needful of translation before.
Mirages, wheat drift, particle match, Brownian
        all this afternoon in the stormy cellar.
I don't know, what did you say?, planet tilting.
And the use of houses, the slam of goddam words for things.
For further surface of my lips, traced to yours.
He built long ramps then to climb and bang his bone
        against the ceiling.
That had nothing to do with, I heard.
The walls decked in flesh tone, sculptor flexing hot
        tube of oil.
This thing that barely goes, that it does not fuck.
That it stands outside, and clues me to, a part of what?
Okay if it moves, but I don't.

I can not wear, you can not slip into, this doesn't
    clothe, it houses.
No matter wilder the sex, this thing will not budge.
You at some time will have to leave the bridges.
Have you not understood?, then you will never know
    whether I have not.
This thing here before me has no reason to stop.

Embarrassing isn't it?, this placing of life
    we call the Raft of Death.
Nothing we make up to say or work encases as well.
I have a gift for you, please take it, a
    component of the crystal mind.
But perhaps you are too cursed in filing away the
    cereal ratios.
Just this, the light does not come from, does not
    come with the weather.
It dials its own futurity, which is a stop time shot.
Were you busy?, you were deviled.
If you are too busy, I hope you are thoroughly evil.
The world came loose from its darkness last night,
    nobody knows this.
I had invaded the flight of the things, but forgot
    when I stopped.
I stepped out on the land, in the sea, in the air,
    and tried the immovable block I had thought out.
Two streams, one you can step in again, the other never.
Lights come to be thought seen deep inside.
In case I can say this, in case I top this,
    in case I'm found at a loss and thrown.
The weather is not bankable, this thing here not sensible.
But I listen out all furthers and shoot to you, say!
Will the final thought be cold to the fingers?
Will the music lie, a stone to my hand?
Amazing how bright you are, how dumb, how unfound.

The need to grasp colors, to follow stitches, to raise sticks.
To operate on rocks, on the sill, in the sun glaze.
I washed water, there is no repetition.
There is thing, one is obliged to follow, to hobble, to hollow.
I screamed at the moon, for not being straight up
      to me, on the center of the land.
I caught the last cattle car to Oshkosh and drilled needles
      through the fenders there, fierce in an inkling.
I wanted to seal the belief in trends, but the only
      tingle buckled beyond the bartering.
See everything loose, and then walk up to the door.
The handle and the dog, they are not written to,
      through the smart air, on monday.
This isbruary, this February, this is a crumpled slip of
      possibility.
The ones who remember you are there, though a trifle short.
My hair has not been cut, my hand only partly sure.
But I thought the certain thing brought to me, and
      one day it was, collision ever since.
And hand to brow, warm with uncut radiance,
      the castle tractor fit on the horizon cow.
Far off when you're filtering through something,
      book to last a dome its fill of carbonation.
Long last light click in the brain after noon.

•

Brings you closer when you see yourself later
otherwise all of it buried in nightbends
when laugh is the closest you'll get to its chew

Someday I'll go to be the glow ghost of itself

•

Insubstantial as friends listed
the pawing of the rain box, the stemming of the snow
but not to be a relief discarded
some day they stay
and you will slot the rest of your days through witnesses
storm heads in sod range
existed as all the crystal stayed
the brain so crossed

●

Insemination of lights into whatever you see
list of capsules in the drain field
harking down to glare cracked clot
I want to hate it, but it fibs me too clear
the notion . . . but of it with it at it to it, no notions.

Sky flake in a water pocket of whim doubt
nothing even barely there would take it
beyond a hole in shred of the task
and the wind whips rain the crystal stumps
I saw seeing what it does that I will
that I station, square
collapse pocket behooving the blues . . .

●

Nothing results from this. The crystal still
on the table. All the words have passed it
and gone here. I give a roaming thought to the matter
which will not be absorbed, nor will an exactness
show. I rant on around and at and wholly past
that thing remains. I neither give to nor take

from it a single. Perhaps I have loosened
its word but a little? A particle.
That it was all too clear to me.

•

Nothing is clear but the ridge road, the eyelet
at the corner of a louvre frame, the uselessness
of things you haven't lived beside and even those that
you have. I have no knowledge I could put my
hand on if I wanted it to hold and turn
a few revolutions in lieu of globe or deepest window.
The track traces itself beyond the sheet. I have those
friends who will always tell me the time. Nothing
has been kept quiet, some of it merely comes quiet.
I look and see, in some obfuscated moments.
Of the salt surely in the sand, not a spark.
The lights to go out so the stars come free.
Nothing is clear but the circular.

•

I wanted to go on seeing the breast, not so much
touching it, though that too is possible, while I went on
in possession of other things. All sides clear, all
surfaces are part of the sex mask, that clasp
one is seeing or touching out from within
to stay hidden while seeing moving grasping reflecting all.
That impossible push, gnash of the convulsive sublime.
A congestion of all falls in time.

Partially masked she is sitting, a blouse opening, her
arms pressed to her sides but her hands
are nowhere. A whisper, a filament of doubt
in the air. And I seem to want to wash
that air with body, by drawing the cloth

across flesh, the opening bars of a strict enough cadence.
Almost all of it over in every flick. The light
across blinds a definite partial of acts that skid.
And I ask of the air the body's impossible breadth.

•

I am overplaying the mark?

Maybe everything is getting too flux for us
and still the evenings
do not, they and all
are in lair, just for just
as true everywhere sun

Dances and car spots the
leaf at the roof of a dial quite
as not true as ever the sud of a wind
hopping instead of drying
your mast, your run hair

Everything as much
a misnomer as is
the caught things, the classroom truce
the making believe it's still
that collection strife
that screw in gumption that strews love

•

"an expanded means of utterance
an overflowing of the meaning"

•

It snows all day, and the lies that are closest to us.
I want it to filter me. I want to be put through . . .
As seeing goes through the trunks. To the
alter-image. Then I am not myself and happily
what I become I see. Through a glass, through
a stone. And to hear only what that thing allows.
Thing is. Not a gloss. To only be shaken out by
the things of the world and the words I read be merely
other things in the struck expanse. I want night.
I want the lights to part and night be alive.
That it matters completely, the singed edges and the
brought tongue. The starling nightmare and the lap
of all construe. Figures that interrupt and are
the arrival. Learning to spell means shunning the
crystal? How to keep to the way out of the way.
Believable crescent across the loggable desk.
Time things.

But wristing interest in what festers, the
loggable dream? The ate face on the lone
tap? How to arrange so all this swills as
it hardens? Snow remote coast shelvage?
Intermittent bomb whistle partita? The glow
of bull agate in a fancier? They ate
regularly, timing. Repetitions of face in the
so told whole oak desk hold. Only one remaining
singer of the lone ranger? And first off told
he was a beamer? This all held in a
post hole of the desk, ground cast I think of.

•

But a piece of writing is not with these words simple.
It tasks and wanes. It is caught on the gadget
of night, and waters. Wrests and twines.
Illuminated cubicle that is gone at a glimpse.

Strangeness and a winning glare. Impossible to see
but speak. Impossible to catch the draught at its
start. And then I think.

And then it cleared, and there was only light.
Light useless for the moment undirected.
What do I see to make an end?
I must change the whole fragiosity of the world, with
this stone? Impossible words. Diurnal
dense immurement in the stational. Coming to
part with the wrong clasp. I open the day with
the crystal and sing to it. With it all things
come tangent to turn and then leave.
And now on nothing to be parsed evenly,
even being the extreme, the lunge.
The wind blows scraps. And those remnants
get titled up. I am asoak in last things
and scream. The work then set, is lost.

A diurnal pressure of dancing, in an avoidal turn
about the room, the page to be absorbed askance.
The glass of water on the table and it is
crystal in a water glass.

It's taking my light? It's taking my words.
A long time to convolve whole. And in here
the night prepares. A cutting edge
starts now.

Where many does not mean a softness.
The explosiveness of a straight piece of felt.
Critical mass of cramped hand.
The body is loose enough, tie it to a single.
But none appears. That nothingness wherein

whatever can be grasped is never the one one
expected to appear, so thereby
does the crystal seem none.

I have made up a procedure here to which
there never can be an end.
Thus the book itself can never sink, but
floats on.
I am number, saith the Lord.

•

As the winter, I have not seen it
as the crystal, it is more spread

Has the house, the hand uncertain
it has me, breaking the spell

The door to the uncertain substances, solid
presents myself with what I do not

Wish, and then dive, and pointing my face
leaving no trace, the subject stands

The while of the crystal, flush, the bulk
of the thing, the ruminal, standing for standing for

My name is object, subject to stand for
the end of its song, a vacuum, a natural

And the missing pieces, they stutter and fall
of parts to the day, to amount without name

It says to myself a number, this in sum
as long as it's sung, is it one?

•

The words roll down under my hand and lock.
What I didn't want. Today is clearly.
But the unparallels wish it streamed. Non-learned.
And even a period crushes the fist, this way of timing.

Only travel allows me stick
to the apparent surface?
Otherwise the mind takes its own powder.

And so does the war come. Again
the crystal will be valuable. A prize
for the rapid if not the wise, in the lengths,
in the night. That this after all all
stays in one place, the crystal its post.
Crazy motion requiring value, and some spot.

The point at which the crystals grow small enough
the turn is away. I could not look
at that rate of returned attention
to results of saturation, the bend
in the glass, the levels of reshuffled
breath spurned me. I will return
only at termination of such
knowledge.

●

These are names drawn from faces in the substitute storm.

Things are balanced, concealed, brooked,
taken as the time it took to enclose
all added things in the head at the head
of a column here typed lying down.
Who do you see as beyond
such things? Where is the "falsehood value"
in a stolen book of whole words?

These words, night and day, luke and cold, slim,
firm, in order of the constellations to
a perfect fix, crystal vase, and not knowing
how to get out of same, things in mind and
faulty drainage, the housing perfectly buried
and after
and firmer, colder, dimmer, in order,
in filter the colors seem older, the wants
on farm or in city stream
bowl us over (a perfect "fit", or human order).

Things are not the same. The age of my name
in a list and at the doorsill of a sexual accounting
score a certainty, a slick hand's portion of the light
one day, precursor of several stones
of no amount, as I have said
in other
(razor in the rain)
terms that occult.

●

     "a succession of stones we are made of
       pale *region where the light is bent*
       has come to resemble not exactly a mountain"

●

There will be no
enumeration of things not
fit here the crystal has erased

No "hand in aid"
no threatening
agglomeration
Do I
remember my own?

Starting from match
the crack in the builded lesson
the overwhelming through
of all held present (a notched
wrist), say what's forgotten

Stay on it, cleaved to
that razor handle
makes of each night
the day before the day
before the said
before the word is sure
(or hinder
the form of a spindle)
the drop before the join

If I say I see nothing
do I see thereby I've nothing said?

And the stone below all
means to state this here

                        •

There was an orange light next to the night light
but then it began to blink. I had thought.
I will. Later two things become the one part
you never want to excuse or explain. Tarsier
with frigid, or broken, hair. The ones from which
we never seemed to glean anything of interest.

The one with the crystal hat, the stone building
with the crystal termination. A library with pyramidal
skylight. The sky is light. The crystal
is a problem of structure. My speech a stricture
in this land where bougie white ones rave.
And this is the theory, which is mine, my theory,
that it is. In the morning road a burning glove.

•

It snows all day, and the closet lies near us.
The back of the hand stirs, follicles and remembrance.
Downhill howls of the shackled hound, the vivid
close to death. Hard to sharpen, near at hand.
This balcony a bouquet, only to mind, only to
trespass, the thoughtful. The saying was, "you've
been a brick", the crystal was, shaken.
Nearest to the end of the snow slope a partita,
refueling, retinged, near to a particular drop.
Every thing in the close beyond a monstrance.

•

The crystal to dwindle not that all I have said continue.
Crystal to crystal word, rule of exaction
exception
my prayer

•

I said
I said and blunt

in sharp and extendibles
to the left
just of reason

Right reason
not mindable
as light is
not "thrown"

It stays
as I say it stays
not my hand

A pistol
the crystal
cunt full of sand

•

To say the snow is all of my mind
to say the trees interruptions
to say the window keeps me
and to keep saying lies
at the base of time

Colder tonight, cold as full tightness, you're brilliant
with glance, with hold, pact of death with detail,
detail with drink, you leave the emptiness
of all else air with silvered me, headful draught

I saw you that
you that would not meet me
slantways in the slow
burn of time, close of cold
fronds of air that sew
thoughts needless, beck of pen
to sorts of light that clasp

You are that baffled star that hides not
slips through the palms' tongues, slivers
and reigns
and I whistle the word no longer
your name

•

In dream scale
I was going toward the place where sticks
would be leaned against the inner door
eyes dry, but upstairs would be the film dark of
                    car drive hall
where to sit with the hiveman of worsted and
          the furious, the implacables in their seat
and here comes my friend who seems
the one to own a hat he's never worn
flown with stripes I'll never see

The honey-wood of slats, the walls of ancient.
the stalls, the store of turmoil-sells, amounts
plain, to arc-blue eyes dry, and I could see the gas
made up in bills of sedge-burn list

This was the brown and blue-burn dream of movement
                    lasted, not enough to beckon
          plot of a ways to shunt
I missed the track of
shown on a rock
a heat has scabbed
this talk forgot

•

We can only live at certain states of tiny activity.
All that matters is the rate of movement.
The crystal and I meet, only in a single mode
of the invisible waves.

•

A dark thing sped up
in the water rose
                    but didn't near?
a fat cat hunts voles under the wall.

The time nothing interrupts
the dream time. And
one is completely thought.

I wouldn't think of holding you down
to a reading of all this, a dreaming of the ground as a bulk
the figures don't light well. The crystal stands
for this mismatch in gap.
Live silent
from this and these, there
and here on out.

•

Dream in which I'm playing in a group
with Lee Konitz (a quartet?) and we've just
done taping a tune. Listening to playback we
discover that a single note by everybody (simultaneously!)
in the whole piece is wrong, will have to be corrected.
Lee says we'll just have to replay that one note
and drop it in at the exact moment on the existing
tape. This seems to me as if it will be

extremely difficult and I look at Lee for
confirmation but his expression, a slight smile,
leaves me no doubt that this is the only way.

●

Remains the rite of one. Through.
The blade itself be thought object.
And all the air you see no bearing.
It stops. It stops. No and.
It does not cease.

●

Going somewhere and not thinking about it, just reading in place.
I lean and hit the ceiling. There is no thought here
but salt block and penitential landmark, or a sinking
land block. My hand turns to ivory or jet,
in tune to walking the grave page. Lighter dreamers
lodge in my other seats. The day turns dial, and
sands and washes, as if tip of stick could light storm.
Knowing somewhere and then leaving it unread, the digits
head for buttons. I turn on my meal and leave the
stone.

No, stones cannot be seen through. Stones cancellations
throughout the blue vent. In the harm of time
I deliberate and match. There is no code unknown
to someone. The door opens and the thithers
come through. The floated matters of no
known cove.
            Words have no safety zone.

●

But she speaks and they all think of belief.
Then she speaks and they all think belief over.
When she speaks next they all think belief
not worth a tumble. And the room all goes
away to no one. Swift elements.
They told all their strives, it all came out.
They all went back, all came again, and
left, clean. Making a breast of it, laughter
and pinched visage, just a cleft in time
A pester way of knowledge. Elbows on shelves,
gum in the machine, discs over the years.
And no central lap but faces voices,
wrapper on their stored plans. Hell yes, any
life collapse blank. Any union well met
for the saying. Life shortened for the staying.

●

Growing tender and thinking
of injections, growing tendency
films that weigh down the
Japanese toupee, hearts askew

Giant tender inkling
whistles when you think about it
top of the zero growing hair
lungs and a full blast tendency

They live there in those silly homes
with window loaves and clear cucumber
as we penetrate off from back of thoughts
back them up and kindle your fingers

I saw a film on the crystal
it was not native but didn't date
badly
oddly I turned
to cracks in the sender

•

It's all just a cardboard release from the edges
of things that doesn't. Where mooning over
heaven won't do. You sigh, then turn in enclosure
over. The meat of winter is staling on the planks.
And there's a minor squirrel fitting in place.
Do we live among hulks, every? The meeting of the
smiles then secondary? Banana on a board and
tearing backdrop? Silence these questives.
I had a hand in turning a further to. A mouse
the cat left for display purposes. A notebook
I followed for glow and decay.

•

It's a cardboard song release. How can I make
strokes as strongly variant as those? It is
now spring. It is not spring. It is a false
chatter. It is an underbolt tingling. The drum is
loose. The first person I see does not speak.
Sky-blue sweaters that do not match in the freeze.
How far away is the coast?, the edge of frozen splinters.
These are notations somewhere between mind and tree.
These thinks he will carry me on. Salad with sherbet
and chair rungs. Bronze cymbals with a throaty tone.
My name gets lost. The door rises and certain things
are gone. All that remains here is an enclosed loss.
Typing paper circles on the moon.

Nothing but stays specific. I dream that I inspect
an old issue of Angel Hair and see there my old poems
are scatters of words circled by drawn birds' wings
and stars, a decorative work, things that urge to
come loose pinned to the page. I can look them up
but I can no longer think them. Nobody sees me
do this. Am I in a long enough room for the
waves to shape right? Maximus
moldings that rust.

•

I read all kinds of novels and don't think I will know
them very long. What is literature in the swirled world?
Emil, asleep, peels a lime. You mustn't type sentences,
they are all loose. Think of nothing but the crystal,
as if sleep were object, insupportable, nonportable.
Think of nothing, or the crystal. It is a handwriting
that will never hold me up. It is a large thing
that takes little space, a crack.

Soon I will stand up from this page and wonder about.
Words allow things that don't much exist beyond them.
Like: the edges of a cloud touch. Pieces of the poem
are all you'll get.
    The edges of a cloud touch.
    Snow ash?
    Lazy blap. Rollercoats.
    And the bars open
    and the stems float out.
Now. Pieces of the poem are all you'll get.

•

I read all the words of novels too and remove them and write them
Write with them. This is the way I would lose them.
If I write with them as well they are gone from me. I perhaps
do not intend this but it is the draw of the process.
Words pulled into sentences and away from me.
I only realize the first moves of this.
I know only the intense starts, which are now dreams.

●

Darknesses that degree as light. And a certain shade
that remains the dream illumination. Backgrounds that are
seen in every detail but edge in like low rumbled sound.
In this seeing is a sort of walking, and thought is muscled.
A huge city grinding that patters in brain linings.
A heaviness at Dakar, binding in Lima. I hold
in the portico and whistle and watch engines absorbing grit streets.
It is pre-dawn and the people await lifts to their works.
They shift before placards and awnings, their expressions
will not click. I step out onto the terrace of
empty tables where are newspapers left and marble stairs
descending, red candies lit where dawn
should come. Where city raises darknesses higher
and I can connect none of my words. Time
has been covered here in background tomorrows
as I may be buried in memory's mass. But I
turn, step within, and the words all run backwards
from this past.

●

Is the heart of poetry a stillness, and my beloved
momentum something else, additional, mongrel?

●

The crystal holds light but is not hollow.
A sweep of the pen does not even cut the page.

•

All
clear
ideas

Tend to be
tended to
end wrongly

The crystal
the vice
of no choice

•

"Move the needle of your radio receiver along the short-wave
band. Between the foreign voices and alien anthems crowding
the invisible frequencies, there stretches a deep gulf. The
gulf is filled with an enormous hissing, and sometimes
a prolonged, humming blare, like wires stretched between
the stars. You are listening then to the size of the world,
and its false, electronic intimacy. You are listening perhaps
to what the Hindus call *ākāsá:* the dark which has no end."

•

And the shadows lean and the people speak and the
faces. The eyes glance, are glanced, open only
to shut. The room is the dream, the shell of
apportionings, the closure of foregrounds. The whole
of the dream, the while of shadow-light, a strict
room. See you across it, lift to death.

Eyes shine the shadows to a duller gong. I could
mix you up with another, is music. Ashes
that do not fall, feels that spill and catch the
floor in maps. Your speech matches nearly
another's lips. Openings sharpen the walls.
You are used by shadows, picked up at edges, lit by the
thresh. The number of the moon could be known, it is written
behind the lamp. You tap me and say,
there is no other door.

25VIII82—9VI83

NOTE

The quotations interspersed through the text were taken from the writings of: André Breton (p. 9), Wallace Stevens (p. 21), Nikola Tesla (p. 26), Louise Brooks (p. 56), Kobo Abe (p. 71), Kobo Abe (p. 83), Yukio Mishima (p. 92), Maurice Blanchot (p. 99), Yukio Mishima (p. 106), Jack Kerouac (p. 109), Philip Whalen (p. 116), Victor Hugo (p. 117), John Ashbery (p. 135), Michael Palmer (p. 140), and C. J. Koch (p. 151).

AFTERWORD

An Interview with Clark Coolidge
on *The Crystal Text*

BY JASON MORRIS AND GARRETT CAPLES

CLARK COOLIDGE: I just realized *The Crystal Text* (1986) is about 40 years old. Because it was written in 1982–83. It's very much a winter book.

JASON MORRIS: How did the crystal come into your possession?

CC: It's funny, I was looking at my notebooks from before and after, since I don't have the crucial one anymore, which is in the Poetry Collection at SUNY Buffalo. The sequence that year is interesting. In June, my wife Susan and I came out here to Healdsburg for a couple weeks, and then I went directly to Boulder for the Kerouac thing [*On the Road: The Jack Kerouac Conference* at Naropa University], which was July of '82. Michael Randall, a lapidary guy I didn't know, had a shop out there. He just handed me the crystal and said, "I understand you like minerals. Take that." At first, I thought, "Oh, I got a million of those." But I didn't want to say anything not thankful, so: "Thanks." Then I thought, "But a guy gave it to me." It was an exchange. Therefore, maybe something's supposed to happen to it, to me, to complete the sequence. That helped me to look at it as something a little more special than just another quartz crystal, which are very common.

I put the crystal in my pocket and carried it home. Then we went down to Martha's Vineyard for a couple weeks. After that, I went back home and started writing this book almost immediately. I must have been thinking about it. I wish I had written more in between, diaristic stuff, but I don't tend to do that. But I did write down the books I was reading, just before I started writing *The Crystal Text*, early August of '82. Bernadette Mayer had just written *Utopia* (1984), and sent it to me. One of my least favorite books of hers—she knew that. That's the one where she thinks nobody should have to pay for their residence or there should be no landlords. It's a real "kill my landlord" book. [Laughs.] A bunch of dreams that came off that. Kind of pissed-off-at-Bernadette dreams. I mean, not *really*.

Then I was reading something by Robert Smithson. I had just written down "Smithson," but I don't know what it was. And this is sort of unusual: I was reading a book by T.E. Lawrence, Lawrence of Arabia, called *The Mint*, which was set after the Arabian campaign. I found it at a used bookstore down on the Vineyard. And Michael McClure's *September Blackberries* (1974). I don't know quite what that has to do with it. But I always think what you're reading right before you write something is important.

JM: You had just written *Quartz Hearts* (1978), right?

CC: Is that right? I had written it before, but I'm not sure. *The Crystal Text* wasn't published until 1986. So maybe something got published in between. It's always a conflict between when you wrote something, and when it gets published. When people begin to see it and react to it. Anyway, I had it written down in my notebook, 29th of July: "and tonight I'm given a quartz crystal." That's all I wrote.

I was looking at my dream notebook to see things that were around that time. This was August 9, '82, right before I started *The Crystal Text*: "B[ernadette]'s *Utopia* made me have that school/exam nightmare again! Complete with having my clothes stolen, or mislaid as they moved & cleared stuff aside for somebody else's exam(room). Meanwhile, I'm involved in a very elaborate exchange of metal 'pods' from forklifts to truck-back fruit-bins & dealings with guys, some kind of black-market scenes, sposed to allow me

to have special treatment on exams, parties and tuxedos where I'm
expected to speak specially to certain ones, etc. It all seems to come
to naught anyway, with"—this mentions a guy named Louis Royal,
who was a classmate of mine—"with Louis Royals ululating in the
semi-darkness. Finally as I'm almost hopelessly giving up & walking
down marble steps & home along Morris Avenue"—where I lived—
"soon it will be revealed to all & my parents too just what a wash
out I am, [another classmate] Steve Salk, calls to me with advice
as to how I should be more 'tearfully' 'Peter, Paul and Mary' about
(around) these exam times. I wake up seeing shining silver imple-
ments all laid out in the wrong order in the wrong boxes/trucks &
it's always inexorably all-over too late! Thanx, Bernadette!"

I don't think that has anything to do with it, but it was funny.
Then this dream August 11, a couple days later: "Barry Watten
insists that he was never kidding about anything, all those years
of Language seriousness—pulls out an old issue of *Change* ([John]
Sinclair's magazine) to show me a group photograph (folds out like
a wall) including himself and Bill Berkson—can't remember the
occasion of significance. Barry couldn't have been part of that: not
old enough—Bill neither, for reasons of association (never knew
Sinclair). The past all a (re)construct . . . But there's Barry all insis-
tent & grown huger in a room."

JM: So those are all from '82. Do any of the dreams relate to the
writing of the text in any way?

CC: Well, there are dreams that are in the text. Like that Lee Konitz
dream, right?

> Dream in which I'm playing in a group
> with Lee Konitz (a quartet?) and we've just
> done taping a tune. Listening to playback we
> discover that a single note by everybody
> (simultaneously!)
> in the whole piece is wrong, will have to be corrected.
> Lee says we'll just have to replay that one note
> and drop it in at the exact moment on the existing

> tape. This seems to me as if it will be
> extremely difficult and I look at Lee for
> confirmation but his expression, a slight smile,
> leaves me no doubt that this is the only way.
> [pp. 145–146]

I really love that dream. That's almost like having that experience.

GARRETT CAPLES: Is the Konitz dream also in the dream notebook?

CC: Yeah, I just copied it from the dream notebook into *The Crystal Text* notebook. I don't think I'd even typed up this collection yet. It was just in notebooks.

JM: Do you still keep a dream journal?

CC: Not as religiously as I once did. I still write 'em down. Lately I've been forgetting dreams a lot. You know that thing, where you wake up and you have the sensation of having a really fantastic, complicated dream, but you can't remember anything about it. You just remember you had it.

JM: So you get back from the Kerouac conference in Boulder and back to New England. *The Crystal Text* is very much a poem dominated by winter. It's begun in the end of summer or early fall, and it leaves off at the end of spring. It's a winter light that seems to filter through the crystal.

CC: I was surprised when I was just looking through *Crystal Text* that it was so heavy with winter references. But then I thought I shouldn't be surprised because we had usually very long and difficult winters there. You could often get snow in October. Even in early June, we did once have six inches of very wet snow, which turned out all the lights and knocked down poles. It's hard to forget extreme weather like that over a period of six months.

JM: I've always thought of the book as a logbook, logging the hours, days. You mentioned at one point that you thought of the sections as "entries."

CC: It was pretty much daily entries in a notebook. It was just a plain fact of, you know, writing a few lines and making a line or dot to pick it up the next day. Start here, continue. That's plainly what the structure was. Within that, of course, there's gotta be things going on that I don't know if I can describe.

GC: Was that your practice at the time, to generate by hand?

CC: Yeah, but it usually wasn't in a notebook. I mean, I would have a notebook going, but it wasn't to directly become the work. It would be quotes and notes—maybe beginnings—what you do in notebook. This is more like a journal, or not quite a diary, but it is in the sense that, for example, it talks about the weather. We were living in a house in what they call the Taconic range, which is a parallel range to the Berkshires, lower hills, mostly in New York state, though our house was in Massachusetts. Living in that house, you couldn't avoid the weather. It was facing west with floor-to-ceiling glass, so all the weather came from the northwest. You'd sit there watching these horrible storms approaching; you couldn't get out of the way.

JM: It has the feel of a captain's book at sea describing various states of weather—both internal and external.

CC: Well that's one of the things going on. It makes me think of that other part of the long book *Book Beginning What And Ending Away* (2013) called "Weathers," where I literally kept a weather journal every day for a month, and then used that as a structure to build the sections, which were pretty much days. That seemed perfect because Bernadette was publishing it in *United Artists* magazine, serialized. She had done [her book] *Memory* (1976), which was like 30 photographs on a day. A page a day for 30 days. I was aware of that. But it's interesting the differences caused by what you do with that little notebook.

JM: You and Bernadette were talking about the idea of the "everything work." Do you think of *The Crystal Text* along those lines as much as you would, for example, *Book Beginning What And Ending Away*?

CC: Of course, that had already been written. *Book Beginning What And Ending Away* was a '70s book. I was looking at the sequence; the book project before I wrote *The Crystal Text* was that thing of mine Lyn Hejinian published, *Research* (1982). I had made a note somewhere, that it had a going-back-to-basics feel, that work. It's all single lines, with spaces between them. *Research*, the word came from Godard. He would say, if somebody criticized his work or he himself criticized it, "I realized I needed to do more 'research.'" It's almost exactly the same word in French, *recherche*. That word struck me; it was a scientific word. Okay, I'll see what happens if I just limit myself to like a simple statement or one line. And try to not be "out there" for the words, but, rather, state something and state something else. There's a certain amount of that in *The Crystal Text*. It starts again and again; when you have these kind of entries, it always has a sense of starting again. The crystal was supposed to ground me that way. Not in any far-out spiritual sense, or even mineralogically.

JM: More as just a device?

CC: Of some sort. To start the day's entry. I had the crystal on a window sill. I was in a basement room where the windows were right at ground level. It was placed right there on the sill, in front of my typewriter. I almost couldn't avoid looking at it. It stayed there for about a year. That's where it was supposed to live. I let myself entertain all kinds of ideas and crazy notions about it. The crystal could do this, it could do that. Or I would think to myself, "Well, I know it couldn't do *that*. It couldn't do that, I couldn't make it do that." But then, "What if it spoke? Maybe the crystal can 'talk' to me." But that's one of the things that it actually told me, which was an impossibility. It slammed the door in my face, which is interesting. As long as stuff like that kept happening, I was pretty happy. Plus, minus, and just keep the exchange going. It's the kind of thing that you can almost continue forever in a way. *The Crystal Text* is full of that kind of self-investigation, dialogue, which I think is what makes it interesting. Otherwise you might just be saying the same thing over and over again.

JM: *The Crystal Text* is limited to the crystal, but it still seems to be an "everything work." The crystal is not even the primary concern of the poem in some ways. It is and it isn't. You describe it at points as a "sky flake in a water pocket," "a lock of standages," "a glow zone," or "a rig of partial light."

CC: I keep trying to describe it in different ways. Totally different ways, if possible. I also noticed, just looking through the book: it starts with a *he*, in the third person. It doesn't really start with the crystal either. It takes a page or two before it says "crystal." That made me wonder, because I can't really remember: did I have the whole setup in my mind to begin with, or did I just start writing in the notebook? I think it was all set. I think I wanted to write the crystal somehow and had the crystal before me. I do a certain amount of jumping around with grammatical persons in the book. But it could be almost a narrative situation with a guy. It begins, "He had his things ready." And it turned out that that isn't what I was gonna do at all. But that is what I ended up doing in a way. The crystal pushed me to bring in other things, it attracted things to itself, or that's my mind working. Bringing up things, because you can't stand to have a vacancy. Even Beckett, I don't think, could stand it for very long.

JM: Beckett is certainly one of your primary influences and his presence seems pretty pervasive to me in *The Crystal Text*. In your sense of humor and also in that starting and stopping, failing, then getting going again.

CC: Fail again. Fail better. Right.

JM: The description of the crystal is a daily task with no end.

CC: I suppose there is some influence, because Beckett is always there for me, so I don't think about it that much. But somewhere in *The Crystal Text*, I say, "Am I like Beckett, except with more things?" Something like that; that's not quite it.

GC: Returning to the notion of the "everything work" you were talking about, was this influenced by post-structuralism? Those writers use the word "text" a lot.

cc: Everything, right. Isn't the word "text" inclusive in some way? Like it could almost include everything? Whether you could or would want to. It's not like any other title I've ever had. It just seemed right for this very focused project. I tend to think of "text" as a French word, which it is, more or less. It's funny because when I went over to do that translation seminar [in Royaumont, France, in 1986], I picked *The Crystal Text* because I figured that they would like that: "Le Texte du Cristal"; it fit their language. And it immediately fell apart on the first page, because they started asking me what the words meant to me. [Laughs.] And I had more than one meaning. It drove some of these guys out of their brain [imitating translators]: "No—I mean, what do you *mean*?"

But I never read those post-structuralist guys, seriously, too much. I tried. Bernadette was more into that than I was. Lacan. She tried over and over to get me to read it and I tried, but I couldn't get anywhere. But she's somebody who had read all of Freud, and loved it, and thought of him as a writer. I would say, "That dream stuff is bullshit." And she would say, "Well the point is that he was a great writer." He was almost like a poet to her. So that's a difference between me and Bernadette.

JM: I was going to ask if you looked at the crystal at different times of day.

cc: Yeah. Because it's a clear prism, so the light is gonna look different or it's gonna do something different to the light, depending on the time. Which is one of the fascinations of it. I figured I had that variable going as well. I began finding out things like that, even after I started. Quartz is one of the most common materials in the world. It's in granite, sand, beach silica. It's all over the place. It seemed right to use something that was kind of a basic building block, although a lot of its forms aren't as pretty as that crystal form.

Of course, this crystal, Michael Randall had buffed off the bottom of it, on a lapidary wheel, so it's rounded. People were really into crystal massage at the time; he was probably gonna sell that as a crystal massage tool. Something I always thought was totally nuts. But then *I'm* using a crystal to write this book!

Most of the things that I've done—that I think a lot of us do as poets—we don't think of as for other people, when we're doing them. Of course, there's all sorts of process after that happens, after you write it. Opportunities, or people you know, or somebody has a magazine. But that's not the basic impulse and it's not there, mostly. The times when it is, are more difficult for me, like writing a blurb. You know what you're doing, why you're doing it. You have to "get it right," in a way. Whereas you don't have to, in the poem. I suppose if I wrote essays, that's almost in that bucket too. "Stick to the subject, Clark!" I'm telling myself sometimes in this work: "Oops, get back to it. You got way off"—which you want to do. But then on the other hand, that particular entry ran out, so let's start again.

JM: There are moments throughout where you're almost chiding yourself to return the focus on the crystal.

CC: That's what I mean. I deliberately put it in front me, right in my sightline, so that I wouldn't be able to avoid it. It's funny; Susan asked me the other day, "What else were you writing at the same time?" I'm sure she's right that it was something, because I tend to work on more than one thing.

JM: I remember you mentioning that some of the poems that were later collected in *Sound as Thought* (1990) were ongoing while you were working on *The Crystal Text*.

CC: I think you're right. I would've said short poems. Or almost occasional poems, but not strictly.

JM: Those poems landed outside *The Crystal Text*, most obviously because they weren't concerned with the crystal.

CC: *The Crystal Text* is a very specific project. I think it probably was fairly easy to keep it separate all the time. Part of my project, ongoing, is poems. Something might have come to me; I might sit down at the desk or wake up in the morning with something, a small poem, type that up, and then go back to *The Crystal Text*. I was writing this by hand, in a notebook. I don't think I typed it until I finished it, which was unusual for me.

GC: Were there parts that you left behind or did you type up everything in that notebook?

CC: I know there are other things that I'd left out. That's why I would've liked to see the MS notebook, to see what I left out. I know I did leave things out. I would have to figure out, "Why wasn't that in there? Why wasn't that as good as the next few inches below?"

JM: Did you move things around or is it chronological?

CC: It's steady. There might be one or two things I moved, but I doubt it. And if there were, they would have been things that were next to each other anyway. I might have thought, well, that looks better first.

JM: It has the feel of running through the seasons that way.

CC: Oh, that's absolutely steady going.

JM: I'm not trying to bring a whole bunch of quotes and ask you to explain them. But there's one that I couldn't resist, which I love: "The crystal is always showing a world / that does not exist except in remission. / It does not contain, but transposes." [p. 37]

CC: I think I was getting desperate. I really wanted something to change. But I had to admit that the poem wasn't doing that. Or that I was trying to describe a process which wasn't there.

GC: What made you feel like you were done writing *The Crystal Text*?

CC: I can't remember. I know that something did. I always get a message with some kind that this is the extent of it. The great example of that was *Mine* (1982) where it ended up with an image by Picasso that I had on my wall from the blue period, with a profile of a woman extending her arm. I don't know whether he described it as an Egyptian image or I thought of it that way. I remember Philip Guston telling me that some other painter of the time called Picasso "an Egyptian painter." Guston thought that was proper, that Picasso was an Egyptian painter. It was almost like Philip wanted to be an Egyptian painter too. Maybe in all those pyramid things that he later did. I remember getting an image while writing *Mine* that stopped me, that somehow said, "Over." It went on; I tried. I wrote another 20 pages and it didn't work. I realized that the instruction was absolutely right. I don't think I've ever had one as direct I did in that case, but with *The Crystal Text* there must have been something that—I don't think it was exhaustion. I think it was just, "You've done enough," or those instructions that I get.

JM: "Transmission complete."

GC: So it took almost a year, but not quite, to generate *The Crystal Text*. It's on its own timeline.

CC: I don't know if I ever thought about limiting it to a calendar year, or anything like that. That was certainly the most forceful time of the year there. Maybe when I survived into another spring, I decided, "Okay, made it one more time." And of course, in winter, you're constantly looking at snow crystals.

GC: It's the season where crystal as such is built into the weather.

CC: That's right. And that thing where they say no two snow crystals are the same. It's always hard for me to believe that, but evidently it's true.

JM: And snow crystals and rock crystal are structured in similar ways. They've got a kind of an architecture.

CC: Well, they're both hexagonal. Water crystals and silicon. That's interesting that they both have the same crystal system. Crystals do have an axis geometrically. You could draw it out, make an axis in different systems. When I wrote that work *Melancolia* (1987), based on the Durer lithograph, it has a polygonal stone form, which that angel was leaning on. Guston had the reproduction of that pinned up on his kitchen wall. We used to talk about it, because there's quite a mystery about that: what is that creature? Is it an angel? Is it the artist? Is it just a human? Nobody will ever know. I built a paper model of that polygonal form, because I wanted to see how many sides it had. I did find out, and then when I wrote the work *Melancolia*; that's as close as I've come to a number fascination. I used a number system based on the number of facets of the polygon, wanting to make myself feel that I had discovered something about Durer, which I probably didn't.

JM: You lived with that lithograph for a long time, front and center like the crystal.

CC: Yeah. Even the little paper model I had. But it was so flimsy that it fell apart. It was just made of thin paper that was taped together. It should have been made out of wood, but I didn't have the capability.

GC: How frequently did you do this? There's a parallel between the writing of *The Crystal Text* and writing *Melancolia*, with the fact that you have a specific object that you're using for generative purposes. Are there other examples of that in your oeuvre?

CC: No. When I started thinking about *The Crystal Text* for this project, I remembered that there was that parallel in writing *Melancolia*.

JM: Maybe your use of the dictionary for *The Maintains* (1974)?

CC: Maybe you can say that's a source too. But of course, with minerals, I finally figured out that's what my interest in geology was. The objects that they are, everything about them. The color, the weight, the density, the transparency or not. Where they come from and the names; they all have these curious names. Some of them are named after the guy who discovered them. Most of 'em are not. "Quartz" actually is described as a German root of unknown origin. There aren't too many words that *Webster's* admits are of unknown origin. So that fascinated me right away. It might be some irreducible substance. And, of course, that'd take me back to Beckett. "Irreducible" is his word. That thing that he told Robert Creeley that night, when they met in Paris at a bar, that he wanted to originate a word? It would be exactly this high, and it would have the substance of stone or something. Oh my God, man, I had the same thought way back when I was a kid. Maybe he did too.

GC: What happens once *The Crystal Text* is done? You write this in 1982 to '83. Once you've typed it up, how does it end up in 1986 being published by Geoffrey Young at The Figures?

CC: I almost want to say it's because he had done some things by me and I'd kind of gotten into his groove. He was probably expecting something kind of long. He might have had the manuscript for a couple of years, for whatever reason, digging up money or something else. I have a feeling the manuscript was "on the roll" for a while. It was about to go into the publishing process, but not immediately because those things usually don't happen with a small press. It turns out he published over a hundred books. I don't know he managed that. The next year, '84, Susan and I went to Rome and Egypt and those books—*At Egypt* (1988) and *Odes of Roba* (1991)—came along. He did those fairly quick, but that might have been through other circumstances. They were inspiring projects to him. Some things I did, I'm sure he kind of gritted his teeth. Then he finally rejected one and that was the end of our publishing relationship, but he did many more than I thought he would ever do. I couldn't blame him. But the rejected MS was that still unpublished prose book *Closer and Darker*.

GC: Was there a notable reception of *The Crystal Text* when it was published?

CC: The most reaction I remember is from readings. Because I did what I usually do, if I have something new and I have to read, I read that. Which has led to me not reading anything too many times. In fact, it was strange when the *Selected* (Station Hill, 2017) came out and I was forced to read early things. That was kind of fun. I remember one reading of *The Crystal Text* at St. Mark's Church and Rudy Burkhardt, who I knew, said, "Hey, really great reading." He sent me a copy of a book of his, as a thanks. Things like that. He had used something from a reading of mine for one of his movies actually, which is called *Good Evening Everybody* (1977). It's like a news framework thing. Somebody did write a work taking off from *The Crystal Text* and published it actually.

JM: Melissa Mack. She wrote a book called *The Next Crystal Text* (2018). It was published by Timeless Infinite Light [whose backlist is now on Nightboat].

GC: *The Crystal Text* itself was reprinted in 1995, only nine years later, by Sun & Moon. Its reputation must have continued to grow.

CC: Evidently. It's kind of like water running underground. I don't follow those things. I don't know how one would, really.

PETALUMA, CA
OCTOBER 16, 2022